Emerging Trends in International Development and Climate Policy

Stephan Klingebiel · Thomas Kalinowski ·
Niels Keijzer
Editors

Emerging Trends in International Development and Climate Policy

A Focus on Korea and Germany

palgrave
macmillan

Editors
Stephan Klingebiel
German Institute of Development
and Sustainability (IDOS)
Bonn, Germany

Thomas Kalinowski
Ewha Womans University
Seoul, Korea (Republic of)

Niels Keijzer
German Institute of Development
and Sustainability (IDOS)
Bonn, Nordrhein-Westfalen, Germany

ISBN 978-3-031-65670-5 ISBN 978-3-031-65671-2 (eBook)
https://doi.org/10.1007/978-3-031-65671-2

This Palgrave Macmillan imprint is published by the registered company Springer Nature Switzerland AG
The registered company address is: Gewerbestrasse 11, 6330 Cham, Switzerland

Contents

Notes on Contributors

R. Melis Baydag, Ph.D. is Postdoctoral Fellow and Lecturer at the Chair of International Politics at Ruhr University Bochum, as well as researcher in the research programme "Inter- and Transnational Cooperation" at the German Institute of Development and Sustainability (IDOS) in Bonn, Germany. Her research interests include domestic politics theories of international relations, international political economy, international cooperation and middle powers.

Songhee Han, Ph.D. is a Senior Researcher at the Institute for Development and Human Security, Ewha Womans University, Republic of Korea, and a steering committee member of the Energy Evaluation Asia Pacific. Her research interests include climate-development dynamics, climate justice, sustainable development, and innovative financing for development.

Brendan Howe is Dean and Professor at Ewha Womans University Graduate School of International Studies, Korea, and President of the Asian Political and International Studies Association. He has held Visiting Scholar positions at the East-West Center (Hawaii), the Freie Universität, Berlin, The University of Sydney, Korean National Defense University, Georgetown University, De La Salle University, Universiti Malaysia Sarawak and Beijing Foreign Studies University. Educated at Oxford University (B.A. hons) University of Kent at Canterbury (M.A.) and

Trinity College Dublin (PhD), his research interests span the governance intersections of security, development and human rights.

Jee Hyo Jeon is an undergraduate sociology student at Ewha Womans University. Her academic interests range from quality education in unequal societies and communities to climate action. Based on her quantitative methodology training, she plans to deepen her qualitative methodology skills with the Department of Cultural Anthropology.

Thomas Kalinowski is a Professor of political science at Ewha Womans University, Seoul, Korea and Senior Fellow at the Research Institute for Sustainability (RIFS)—Helmholtz Centre Potsdam, Germany. Recent publications include works on the political economy of financial crisis and crisis management, sustainable governance, the political economy of climate change, the Green Climate Fund (GCF), sustainable governance, the diversity of capitalism and the transformation of the East Asian developmental state. His book *Why international cooperation is failing: How the clash of capitalisms undermines the regulation of finance* was published as a paperback by Oxford University Press in 2022, and his latest article on the "Green Climate Fund and private climate finance" has just been published as open access in *Climate Policy* 2024/3).

Hanna Kang is a Researcher at the National Institute of Green Technology of Korea, where her primary focus lies in the realm of policy development and evaluation aimed at fostering green financing linkages. Before her current role, she was a researcher at the Korea Environment Institute and the Leibniz Institute of Ecological Urban and Regional Development (IOER) in Germany. Her research expertise spans a diverse array of fields, encompassing sustainable urban transition and international development cooperation. She holds her doctoral degree in environmental urban development from Technische Universität Dresden in Germany.

Minah Kang, Ph.D. is a Professor in the Department of Public Administration, Ewha Womans University Kang, Minah (PhD). She is currently the president of the KAIDEC (Korean Association of International Development and Cooperation). Until recently, she served the Korean government as the first female Commissioner of the Board of Audit and Inspection, the Supreme Audit Institution of Korea. She is a member of the Editorial Board of the Journal of Health Systems & Reform and Associate Editor of BMC Health Services Research. She completed a PhD in

Health Policy from Harvard University, Masters of Public Policy from Harvard Kennedy School and BA from Ewha Womans University.

Moon Jung Kang is a Senior Researcher at the National Institute of Green Technology Korea since 2017. She actively contributes to international collaborative projects in climate technology, policy research and UNFCCC negotiations. With a PhD in Innovation Economics from the Technical University of Berlin, she has nine years of prior experience at Korea Institute of Science and Technology Europe, specializing in international cooperation projects in environmental policies and technologies before joining NIGT.

Niels Keijzer, Ph.D. is a Senior Researcher and Project Lead based at the German Institute of Development and Sustainability (IDOS) in Bonn, Germany. In 2022 he was a visiting researcher at Ewha Womans University in Seoul, Korea. He holds a Ph.D. from Radboud University Nijmegen (the Netherlands) based on a doctoral dissertation on the European Union's development policy. His research and advisory work focuses on European development cooperation, external evaluations, aid and development effectiveness, policy coherence for development and financing for development.

Eunju Kim is Assistant Professor at the College of Social Science, Hansung University, Seoul, South Korea. She was a research fellow at the Korea Institute of Public Administration, a national research institute and a visiting fellow at the Centre for the Study of Poverty and Social Justice, University of Bristol, UK. Her research interests include international development policy, global governance, policy evaluation and social protection in developing countries.

Tae Kun Kim is a Sociologist and Principal Researcher at the National Institute of Green Technology. His research focuses on international cooperation in tackling the climate crisis, including cooperation with ASEAN, US and China's policies, science diplomacy, strategies for international cooperation in technology, and Green New Deal ODA.

Stephan Klingebiel, Ph.D. is Head of the "Inter- and Transnational Cooperation" programme at the German Institute of Development and Sustainability (IDOS), Visiting Professor at the University of Turin (Italy), an Honorary Distinguished Fellow at the Centre for Sustainability, O. P. Jindal Global University (India), and Visiting Professor at Ewha

Womans University, Graduate School of International Studies (GSIS). He was Director of the UNDP Global Policy Centre in Seoul, Republic of Korea (2019 to 2021) and Founding Director (2007–2011) of KfW Development Bank office in Kigali (Rwanda).

Donmin Lee is a Senior Researcher at the National Institute of Green Technology in South Korea. His research focuses on international cooperation in the technical evaluation of renewable energy technologies, such as waste-to-energy and biomass-to-energy, to provide suitable technologies and support developing countries in achieving their NDC.

Jooyeon Moon is a Researcher at the National Institute of Green Technology of Korea, where she focuses on the facilitation of climate technology cooperation project operating in overseas countries. Prior to joining NIGT, she worked for UNESCAP in Bangkok in the Space Application Section of Disaster Risk Management Division as consultant. At NIGT, she has participated in diverse projects: waste-to-energy project in Indonesia, solar resource development in Sri Lanka, establishment of a waste separation facility in Bhutan, development of REDD+ policy framework in Samoa, etc. She holds a master's degree in Environmental Science and Ecological Engineering from Korea University.

Min Jee Oh is a Ph.D. student at the Department of Management & Global Business, Rutgers University. She was a visiting researcher at the German Institute of Development and Sustainability (IDOS) from July to September 2022.

Min Joung Park, Ph.D. is an Adjunct Professor at the School of Global Service at Sookmyung Women's University, Seoul. She also works for the Heinrich Böll Foundation, East Asia Regional Office in Seoul, as a Programme Manager for Foreign and Security Policy. She holds a PhD from Ewha Womans University based on a doctoral dissertation on South Korea's development policy towards ASEAN. Her research and advisory work focuses on South Korea's development cooperation policy and practices.

Jale Tosun, Ph.D. is a Full Professor of Political Science at Heidelberg University, Germany, and Adjunct Professor at the University of Oslo, Norway. She is the editor-in-chief of the Nature Portfolio Journal *Climate Action* and an associate editor of *Policy Sciences*. Her research focuses on the governance of climate change, the environment and sustainability, and on policymaking in the European Union.

List of Figures

List of Tables

CHAPTER 1

Introduction: Germany and Korea as Partners in International Development and Green Transitions

Stephan Klingebiel, Thomas Kalinowski, and Niels Keijzer

Abstract This chapter introduces the book and its three parts, which explore the alignment of global sustainable development priorities between Germany and the Republic of Korea. Notably, both nations share a common commitment to development policy and international climate action, an alignment that holds immense potential for enhanced cooperation in today's evolving global landscape. Germany's historical role as a founding member of the international development cooperation

S. Klingebiel (✉) · N. Keijzer
German Institute of Development and Sustainability (IDOS), Bonn, Germany
e-mail: stephan.klingebiel@idos-research.de

N. Keijzer
e-mail: niels.keijzer@idos-research.de

T. Kalinowski
Graduate School of International Studies, Ewha Womans University, Seoul, Korea
e-mail: tkalinowski@ewha.ac.kr

S. Klingebiel et al. (eds.), *Emerging Trends in International Development and Climate Policy*,
https://doi.org/10.1007/978-3-031-65671-2_1

system juxtaposes with Korea's more recent entry into the Organisation for Economic Co-operation and Development (OECD) and its Development Assistance Committee (DAC) in 2010. Korea has transformed from a significant development assistance recipient to an active provider, a transition mirrored in its engagement in international climate finance.

Keywords Development policy · Global sustainable development · Development · International cooperation · Climate change · Developing countries · Global South · Germany · Republic of Korea

Convening a German–Korean Development Research Network

This edited volume brings together development scholars from Germany and the Republic of Korea (referred to throughout this volume as Korea) to identify commonalities and differences in the approaches and priorities of both countries to pursue and support global sustainable development. While different in scope, focus and theme, the contributions share a common objective for Korean and German development scholars to learn from one another.

Contributions to the book were selected from inputs by a wide range of participants to three workshops held at Ewha Womans University, Graduate School of International Studies (GSIS) in Seoul (22 June 2022 and 12–13 June 2023) and at the German Institute of Development and Sustainability (IDOS) in Bonn (17–18 October 2022). These three workshops were supported by the German Research Foundation (Deutsche Forschungsgemeinschaft; DFG) and the Korean National Research Foundation (NRF) in the context of a joint DFG and NRF research grant on "Towards Inclusive Multilateralism: Investigating Synergies in Development Cooperation between the Republic of Korea and Germany", led by Thomas Kalinowski and Stephan Klingebiel. In addition to acknowledging the financial support that enabled the exchanges within the network and this resulting volume, the editors also extend their gratitude to the Ewha Graduate School of International Studies' Institute for International and Area Studies (IIAS), the Ewha Frontier 10–10 programme, the Korea Association of International Development and Cooperation

(KAIDEC) and the German Institute of Development and Sustainability (IDOS) for providing support for the workshops.

Structure and Contributions to This Volume

The volume is divided into three parts. In the first, authors identify shared goals and discuss different policies in development cooperation and green transitions. The second part examines the geopolitical and regional contexts for German and Korean international relations. Finally, the third part investigates current and potential pathways of cooperation between Germany and Korea.

Part 1: Shared Goals and Distinct Paths

Germany and Korea share the goal of an ecologically sustainable future. At the same time, their paths towards sustainability are quite different, providing important lessons for countries in the Global North and the Global South alike. Both countries also share the same vision of a world free from poverty and are the main proponents of international cooperation based on multilateralism. Germany was a founding member of the international development cooperation system as we know it today; Korea became a member of the Organisation for Economic Co-operation and Development (OECD) in 1996 and of its Development Assistance Committee (DAC) in 2010, and is considered both an important former recipient, with incoming development cooperation significantly influencing the country's development, and a current provider of development cooperation. Their different starting points and histories translate to different external expectations and self-perception of their role in the global development system. Their pattern of growth in the provision of official development assistance (ODA) is also different, with a gradual increase for Korea, while for Germany a recent rapid increase to the status of the second largest bilateral provider in the OECD world will probably be followed by a period of decline starting in 2025.

The countries' roles in relation to international climate finance also differ. Under the Kyoto Protocol (1997), Korea was categorized as a Non-Annex 1 country that is not obliged to contribute to climate finance in support of the Global South under the United Nations Framework Convention on Climate Change (UNFCCC). In practice, however, Korea has become a climate finance donor both bilaterally as well as in the Green

Climate Fund (GCF). The first part of the book consists of four chapters that explore various aspects of the above developments, as well as looking at recent policy evolutions.

Germany and Korea: Comparing Systems, Policies and Cooperation Patterns (Niels Keijzer, Stephan Klingebiel and Min Jee Oh).
The Political Economy of German and Korean Sustainability Transitions (Thomas Kalinowski).
Positions of Established and Emerging Powers Towards Climate Finance: The Cases of Germany and Korea (Melis Baydag).
Realizing the Women, Peace and Security Agenda Through Foreign Aid: A Comparative Analysis of Korea and Germany (Min Joung Park).

Part 2: Regional and Global Contexts

The development policies and operations of Germany and Korea are confronted by a challenging global geopolitical and economic setting, as well as a worrying decline in human development globally. Both countries are being challenged to respond to this changing setting and to communicate such changes effectively in their contributions towards advancing sustainable development at home and through international (development) cooperation. Although Korea and Germany have considerable bilateral development budgets and delivery systems of their own, both countries also strongly focus on working within various global and regional alliances, ranging from the European Union (EU) to the United Nations (UN).

This part of the book discusses the dynamic geopolitical context for both countries (for example, the recent Indo-Pacific focus in international relations), the evolving development policy profiles of Korea and Germany, the involvement of both countries in key international organizations and the European Union, their respective roles in international climate policies and entry points for deepening Korean-German cooperation.

The following three chapters deal respectively with the increasing relevance to geopolitics of the development policies of Germany and Korea, including those co-shaped by Germany within the European Union, as well as a focus on the multilateral involvement of both countries. The part focuses also on multilateral solutions to climate justice.

The Impact of Geopolitics on the Field of Development in Korea and Germany (Brendan Howe/Stephan Klingebiel).
The Southernization of the EU's Development Policy? A Critical Review of the EU Global Gateway (Niels Keijzer).
Multilateralism and Climate Justice (Songhee Han, Minah Kang, Jale Tosun).

Part 3: Exploring Collaborations and New Actor Constellations

One key element of the 2030 Agenda and its Sustainable Development Goals is the considerable emphasis it places on delivering lasting results through multi-stakeholder partnerships. The agenda includes specific commitments to revitalizing the global partnership by "bringing together Governments, civil society, the private sector, the United Nations system and other actors and mobilizing all available resources".

This part of the volume includes contributions that review experiences in government efforts to strengthen the role of the private sector in promoting global development. Moreover, it notes that the 2030 Agenda for Sustainable Development is not a set of ready-made solutions but in part includes policy dilemmas and crises that require further assessment and evidence-based solutions. Knowledge actors and research partnerships play key roles in this regard. This third and last part features three chapters that explore the role of various non-state actors in the international cooperation activities of Korea and Germany, with a focus on research cooperation and private sector engagement.

A Comparative Analysis of Korea and Germany's Climate Change Mitigation Efforts: Implemented Technology and Financial Mechanism Projects Under the UNFCCC (Tae Kun KIM, Jee Hyo JEON, Donmin LEE).
The Evolution of Research and Partnership Activities in Support of Urban Transformation: The EU's Research and Innovation Framework Programme (Hanna Kang, Moon Jung Kang, Jooyeon Moon).
Private Sector Engagement Policies in South Korea: Challenges and Policy Suggestion (Eunju Kim).

PART I

Shared Goals and Distinct Paths

CHAPTER 2

Germany and Korea: Comparing Systems, Policies and Cooperation Patterns

Niels Keijzer, Stephan Klingebiel, and Min Jee Oh

Abstract Although geographically distant, there is considerable convergence in the development policy priorities of Germany and the Republic of Korea (hereafter referred to as Korea)—and indeed scope for cooperation between them. Whereas Germany was a founding member of the Organisation for Economic Co-operation and Development (OECD) and its Development Assistance Committee (DAC), Korea joined the DAC more recently in 2010 as an important former recipient as well as a current provider of development cooperation. Both countries maintain a centralized political responsibility for development policy—in Germany's case with a dedicated ministry, whereas in Korea, two ministries share the responsibility for development cooperation. With various line ministries

N. Keijzer (✉) · S. Klingebiel
German Institute of Development and Sustainability (IDOS), Bonn, Germany
e-mail: niels.keijzer@idos-research.de

S. Klingebiel
e-mail: stephan.klingebiel@idos-research.de

M. J. Oh
Rutgers School, Piscataway, NJ, USA

S. Klingebiel et al. (eds.), *Emerging Trends in International Development and Climate Policy*,
https://doi.org/10.1007/978-3-031-65671-2_2

and organizations with implementing mandates involved in both countries' development cooperation systems, fragmentation is a challenge and raises questions about issues that include results reporting, the introduction and use of standard indicators, independent evaluations, consistent official development assistance (ODA) reporting and ensuring effective cooperation.

Keywords Development policy · Development cooperation · ODA · Germany · Republic of Korea · OECD · SDGs

Introduction

This chapter analyses current development policy trends in Germany and Korea. It explores prospects for further changes in policy and for intensifying cooperation between the two countries. Although they may appear to be unlikely partners due to the considerable geographic distance between them, both countries are export-driven and energy-dependent economies that have thrived during times of relative global stability. Germany's identity is closely related to that of the European Union (EU) as well as defined by its close ties with the US. Korea's most relevant political and security ally is the US, while neighbouring China dominates its economic relations. With starkly different outcomes, both countries, moreover, share the experience of having been divided during the Cold War. Overall, they are important development cooperation actors and strong supporters of multilateral approaches.

Seven years since the adoption of the 2030 Agenda and its 17 Sustainable Development Goals, multiple crises have contributed to a situation in which human development declined across the globe in 2020 and 2021, thus erasing the gains made in the preceding five years. These challenging human development trends are taking place in a world characterized by strained international relations, leading to constrained global cooperation. The relationship between Western countries and China—and the latter's more pronounced global ambitions—is a main driver of the shrinking room for global collective action. Geopolitical considerations appear to be increasingly dominating all areas of international politics (Klingebiel, 2022). The Russian invasion of Ukraine is a different and an additional game changer. The aggression is in sharp contrast to international law—especially the Charter of the United Nations (UN). It will have a fundamental and long-lasting impact on global cooperation and multilateralism. This includes the UN as well as "mixed club" governance platforms such as the G20, while leaving some potential for "like-minded clubs" such as the G7 and the OECD.

Our central argument is that in today's challenging geopolitical context, although they may be perceived as unlikely partners by some, Germany and Korea stand to benefit from exploring opportunities for further dialogue, mutual learning and cooperation. Such deepened cooperation would have the potential to complement and reinforce the existing partnerships and groupings through which they engage. In the following sections, we further explore this potential by comparing the origins of development cooperation, contrasting recent budgetary choices and policy priorities, as well as describing respective institutional setups. On this basis, we identify and discuss a range of areas and topics where further cooperation could be focused.

German and Korean Development Policy: Origins and Foundations

Germany and Korea have followed distinct trajectories in order to become the international cooperation actors that they are today. Whereas the Federal Republic of Germany was a founding member of the OECD/DAC (1961) and has more recently grown to become the second largest bilateral development cooperation provider worldwide, Korea is a recent member (1996 and 2010 respectively) and has been regarded as—and presented itself as—a case for effective development cooperation. Germany's Western allies encouraged it to use the socio-economic potential it gained in the 1950s and 1960s to contribute to the bipolar rivalry between the Eastern and Western blocs. The Cold War conditions were thus a key factor in the establishment and evolution of Germany's development cooperation system. Korea's motivation to enter into the field of development cooperation originates from the same period, as it was in part a response to the Democratic Republic of Korea's attempt in the 1970s to gain international support in the developing world by providing development support to some countries (Song & Kim, 2022). This explains how Korea's current approaches find their origins in the country's experience as a South–South cooperation provider, as well as its role as a "bridge" between such providers and OECD members—a function it has successfully fulfilled since 2011, as host to the High Level Forum on Aid Effectiveness in Busan in that year, for example, and subsequently as the regular host of the Busan Global Partnership Fora.

Korea's own development trajectory over the last three decades has been considerably faster and more transformational than all other OECD members. Its post-Korean War period as a developing country is vividly remembered by generations in the country. Thus, the process of "development" is recognized and valued in the country as a recent and "lived" experience. The year 2010 was a turning point regarding development cooperation—the country completed its transition from a former recipient to a key provider of international cooperation. The achievement was marked by its membership of DAC and by the UN Development Programme (UNDP) closing its office as a "country programme country office" that same year (Hong & Izmestiev, 2020; Kwon, 2022). In the years leading up to DAC membership, Korea applied development cooperation as a key means to strengthen its international position and soft power, with the country providing the Secretary-General of the UN in 2007 and becoming the base for the Green Climate Fund (GCF) in 2012. In 2022, newly elected President Yoon Suk-Yeol defined Korea as a "global pivotal state" and emphasized its mission to promote freedom, peace and prosperity based on its liberal democratic values, and invest in international cooperation to this end. Thus, development cooperation continues to be explicitly seen and pursued as an instrument to increase the soft-power capacity of the country.

Korea's own development successes were achieved during a period when the country was receiving considerable levels of development finance, mainly from the US, Japan and multilateral institutions, including the UN development system. The transformation of the country into what it is today has brought about a strong demand in developing countries to learn from Korea's development experiences. Knowledge exchange platforms and institutions such as the Korea Institute for International Economic Policy and UNDP's Seoul Policy Centre play an important role as entry points for other countries interested in policies and best practices (Kwon, 2022; Song & Kim, 2022).

Based on its own development experiences and in a similar way to that of other countries in the region (e.g. Japan and China), Korea gives industrial development and physical infrastructure a high priority. This focus is visible in its policies and public communications. European donors have placed new emphasis on infrastructure only in recent years, with one prominent initiative being Europe's Global Gateway initiative, while Germany has also placed a key emphasis on infrastructure investment in its capacity within the G7 Presidency. Korea's development policy, on the other hand, has been premised on a co-prosperity concept from the beginning, with direct economic benefits being an explicit objective. Similar approaches are used by Japan as a DAC member and China as the most significant provider of South–South cooperation (Kwon, 2022). DAC donors from beyond the East Asia region have typically been less explicit about co-benefits, although here too "mutual benefit" type objectives are increasingly being made explicit in overarching policy statements.

Budgets, Policy Choices and Priorities

Germany's official development assistance (ODA) budget is around 10 times that of Korea's, in part due to—though not fully owing to—its larger population and economy. Yet both countries have in common that they have seen considerable increases in the size of their ODA budgets during the past decade. Table 2.1 presents comparative figures on development cooperation in both countries, reflecting the situation in the first year of the COVID-19 pandemic. ODA figures for 2022 show sustained growth in German ODA to 0.85% of its GNI (USD 35.8 million) and Korean ODA to 0.17% of its GNI (USD 2.8 million). A key difference is linked to the war in Ukraine, with in-country refugees representing 13.5% of Germany's ODA in 2022 while only accounting for 0.4% of Korean ODA.

New governments took to the stage in Germany and Korea in, respectively, December 2021 and May 2022, with both facing the challenge of setting new directions in volatile global and domestic contexts. Germany announced initial "headline objectives" for development policy priorities under the new government, which are expected in a few months for Korea, yet the aforementioned volatile global context presents a considerable number of open policy questions for both countries and complicates the process of defining longer-term policy priorities. Both countries' societies are characterized by adequate public support for development policy, combined with relatively low levels of public debate and broad cross-party support for the policy areas. Recent surveys show that 76% of Korean and 55% of German respondents generally support the countries' ODA budgets and development cooperation engagement, which in the case of

Table 2.1 Comparing recent ODA trends (data for 2022 and 2021)

	Germany	*Korea*
ODA (million USD) (2022)	36.4	2.9
ODA as a percentage of GNI (%) (2022)	0.85	0.17
Percentage of ODA spent in LDCs (%) (2022)	14	33
Top five recipient countries (2021)	India, China (People's Republic of), Syrian Arab Republic, Afghanistan, Jordan	Bangladesh, Philippines, Colombia Cambodia, Vietnam
Country-programmable aid (%) (2021)	38.9	80.5
Percentage of aid non-allocable to countries (%) (2021)	50.4	16.4
Percentage of bilateral ODA provided to and through NGOs (%) (2021)	Support to NGOs: 4.3 Through NGOs: 8.0	Support to NGOs: 0.0 Through NGOs: 1.8

Source Authors' compilation based on OECD data (OECD, s.a.)

Germany shows a relative decline in 2023 with earlier years showing close to 70% of respondents to be in favour (Lee et al., 2021; Morini, 2023).

Germany's current social-democratic-led coalition government between the Green and the liberal parties entered office on 9 December 2021. Among other key changes, it included the first new chancellor in almost 16 years, a three-party coalition and the first change in development minister in two legislative periods. As the former environment minister had done under the previous government, the current development minister introduced four main priorities for German development cooperation: (i) addressing the structural causes of hunger, poverty and inequality, (ii) providing socially fair responses to the global challenge of climate change within the framework of a Just Transition, (iii) avoiding future pandemics and being better prepared with functioning health systems should the worst happen, and (iv) implementing a feminist development policy to eliminate structural inequalities and discrimination. Germany's government has also committed to considerably increasing the provision of international climate finance during the coming years. Key policy initiatives to date concern an ambitious new Africa strategy and a Feminist Development Policy, both published in the first months of 2023 (on the latter policy, see the contribution by Park in this volume).

Although Germany's coalition agreement commits to providing 0.7% of its GNI as ODA, as well as 0.2% of its GNI to least developed countries in this context, the aforementioned crises put considerable pressure on its budget. Following the parliamentary budgeting process, BMZ's budget for 2023 was determined at EUR 12.2 billion, EUR 190 million less than the ministry's budget in 2022. Following challenging discussions linked to the constitutional court's rejection of the government's decision to derogate on its constitutional "debt break", challenging discussions in the coalition government resulted in the decision to set the ministry's budget at EUR 11.22 billion (2024), with further cuts to be made during the next year (mid-term financial planning). Since discussions are ongoing on austerity measures in the government's budget, as well as continuing opposition to other measures announced by groups in society, further cuts may be introduced. This requires the government and relevant stakeholders to justify the country's ODA and the returns it produces.

The Russian invasion of Ukraine in February 2022 prompted strong and far-reaching reactions from the German federal government, including through its development policy. Among other aspects, the invasion affected the development minister's interactions with her European colleagues in various EU meetings, as well as her engagement with the G7 under the German Presidency. In 2022, 13.5% of Germany's ODA budget was spent on in-country refugee costs, a large part of which was linked to Ukrainian refugees based in Germany. The invasion also led to considerable changes to the previous German federal budget and an increased focus on Ukraine as well as the global food security implications of the invasion.

The Korean administration, headed by President Yoon, came to office on 10 May 2022 after a close presidential election. Since this conservative candidate won the election, its effects have rippled out to the local elections as well as the appointment of the new prime minister, Han Duck-Soo, who carries the political responsibility for, and leadership of, Korea's development cooperation. At the 46th Committee for International Development Cooperation (CIDC) held on 30 June 2023, he stated that even in these taxing times amidst the pandemic and polycrisis, Korea's development cooperation would continue to grow stronger under his administration. This was also backed by President Yoon's address on 20 September 2023 at the UN General Assembly, where he stated that such a focus on development cooperation will be championed by an increase in the ODA budget of 40% in 2024 compared to that of 2023, with a focus on realizing global values that entails the promotion of humanitarian values, the strengthening of international cooperation ties, and the realization of mutual and inclusive national interests through strategic ODA.

As presented in Korea's Annual ODA Plan for 2024, announced in June of 2023, the country intends to increase its ODA volume and has proposed a total budget of approximately EUR 4.7 billion (KRW 6.8 trillion) for 2023, which is a 43.2% increase from that of 2022 (EUR 3.4 billion). This would continue the ODA growth path of the previous administrations, with Korea's ODA budget growing at an average rate of 11% per year since it joined the DAC. Moreover, the plan puts particular focus on (i) humanitarian response to global polycrisis, (ii) support for innovation in developing countries through landmark package projects, (iii) reinforcement of partnerships through foreign policies such as the Indo-Pacific Strategy and the Busan Initiative, which is a project linked to Busan's bid to host the 2030 World Expo that emphasizes international cooperation and Korea's role in addressing global challenges, and (iv) effective systemization and management of ODA. If this plan is fully implemented, which is expected to be reviewed by Ministry of Economy and Finance (MOEF) and the National Assembly by January 2024, Korea's ODA as a percentage of GNI will rise to 0.25%.

Starting with the onset of the COVID-19 pandemic in late 2019, unforeseen external calamities have struck Korea as well as the rest of the world, which have prompted changes in development cooperation. The Russian invasion of Ukraine, the escalation of the Israeli–Palestinian conflict (with the Hamas attacks on 7 October 2023), and other unceasing conflicts in Afghanistan, Ethiopia and Syria have brought the need for additional humanitarian assistance, which is reflected in Korea's actions to increase the proportion of its humanitarian aid budget. Compared to 2023, which emphasized the sectors of transportation (13.1% of 2023 ODA budget), health (12.9%), and humanitarian aid (11.0%), in 2024, there has been a significant increase in humanitarian aid (20.6% of the 2024 ODA budget), transportation (14.3%) and health (8.0%).

Furthermore, as announced in the Korean Green New Deal of 2021, ODA will become even more important as climate crisis issues become more significant. Under this strategy, the government expects to significantly expand the proportion of Green ODA to exceed the OECD DAC average (28.1%) to strengthen support for the green transition of developing countries by 2025. In line with the aforementioned strategies, another priority for the new development plans is addressing the food crisis inflicted by both supply chain disruptions and climate change by cooperating closely with the UN, the World Food Programme and the Food and Agriculture Organization. Other priorities include strengthening partnerships with other development actors such as civil society, non-governmental organizations (NGOs) and academia; innovating projects and programmes by embracing digital, ICT and AI development; and strengthening development systems that will encourage knowledge-sharing and systemize performance management.

Organizational Approaches and Structures

The organizational approaches and structures for ODA management differ strongly between the Germany and Korea, both of which have made efforts to address organizational fragmentation (Table 2.2).

The German development cooperation system includes a self-standing ministry in charge of development cooperation: BMZ, which was established in 1961. As a dedicated development ministry, Germany's BMZ stands out from the development ministries of other DAC member countries, yet its coordination mandate is rather "soft". In addition, other federal ministries using ODA resources from the national budget are quite important as well. This, for instance, includes the budget for humanitarian assistance that is managed by the Foreign Office. The 2021 DAC Peer Review of Germany reported that BMZ provides 50% of Germany's gross ODA, while 13 other federal ministries provide around 19% and the rest is managed by the 16 federal states, financial cooperation agencies and various other areas of expenditure. Another key feature of the German development cooperation system is the strong position of its two main implementing agencies: KfW Development Bank and the Deutsche Gesellschaft für Internationale Zusammenarbeit (GIZ). KfW Development Bank is in charge of Germany's financial cooperation in terms of large grants, loans and investment promotion, whereas GIZ is responsible for implementing various forms of technical cooperation that, among other goals, seek to contribute to capacity development.

Table 2.2 Organizational structures of ODA management in Germany and Korea

	Germany	*Korea*			
General coordination	Federal Minister for Economic Cooperation and Development	Committee for International Development Cooperation (CIDC) *Chairperson: Prime Minister* *Members: Ministers of relevant ministries and civil experts*			
Policy and supervision	The Federal Ministry for Economic Cooperation and Development (BMZ): *Overall coordination, reporting*	Foreign Office: *Humanitarian aid* Other line ministries: *Some climate finance and other ODA expenditure*	Ministry of Foreign Affairs: *Oversees grant aid*	Ministry of Economy and Finance: *Oversees concessional loans*	
Implementation	Deutsche Gesellschaft für Internationale Zusammenarbeit (GIZ): *Technical cooperation*	KfW Development Bank: *Financial cooperation*	Korea International Cooperation Agency (KOICA)	Korea Eximbank; Economic Development Cooperation Fund (EDCF)	Other implementing ministries, agencies and local governments

Source Authors

The Committee for International Development Cooperation (CIDC), established in 2006 and chaired by the Prime Minister of Korea since 2022, ultimately guides and makes decisions on Korea's development cooperation policies, and works to ensure that the involved ministries and agencies operate in a coordinated way. At the implementation level, each ministry can operate its own ODA projects, but the two pillars of Korea's ODA are the Ministry of Foreign Affairs—with its implementing agency called Korea International Cooperation Agency (KOICA) overseeing grant aid—and the Ministry of Economy and Finance, through its Economic Development Cooperation Fund (EDCF), in charge of concessional loans. In contrast to GIZ and KfW, KOICA and the Export–Import Bank of Korea (Korea Eximbank), which is in charge of the EDCF, are both staffed by civil servants.

In recent years, Germany's development policy has put considerable emphasis on bringing investment—and notably German companies—to developing countries, with a key focus on small- to medium-sized enterprises (SMEs). Notably, since the 2017 G20 Presidency, Germany has introduced various funds and initiatives, seeking to promote external investment, with a specific focus on the private sector and the African continent. Linked to its bilateral, G20 and G7 engagements, Germany is also a major proponent of the EU's Global Gateway initiative that seeks to strengthen the EU's external investment in the area of soft and hard infrastructure (see Chapter 6 by Keijzer). The Korean government appears to have similar ambitions, as Korea's Ministry of SMEs and Startups has proposed a more than tripled ODA budget in 2024, increasing significantly from approximately USD 3.8 million in 2022, with the main goal of promoting sustainable economic development in cooperation with SMEs and startups in developing countries such as Uganda, Laos, Indonesia, Vietnam, Colombia and Mexico through multilateral channels. Moreover, other ministries and agencies have also recognized the importance of the role of SMEs in the socio-economic development of both Korea and the partner countries. This has placed special attention on cooperation in this field in terms of sharing knowledge, building technological capacities and providing consultations for development.

With the implementation of the Strategic Plans, which started in 2010 and are updated every five years, Korea selects priority partner countries and formulates Country Partnership Strategies that consider each individual country's ODA volume, priority areas and national development strategies to improve aid effectiveness. According to Strategic Plan 2021–2025, Korea selected 27 priority partner countries (12 countries in Asia, 7 in Africa, 4 in Latin America and 2 in the Middle East) out of 130 partner countries, and aims to channel at least 70% of total bilateral ODA to these countries. This has been reflected in the Annual ODA Plan for 2024, and Korea will continue to focus primarily on Asia (38.5%), Africa (19.4%), and Latin America (7.5%), especially to low- and middle-income countries.

Germany's reform strategy "BMZ 2030", decided on in June 2020, introduced a focus on 65 partner countries. The country list consists of three main categories: 47 bilateral partners (including seven "reform partners" with a significant cooperation offer), eight "global partners" (cooperation on shared global challenges) and 10 "nexus and peace partners" (conflict-affected and fragile states). In addition, German cooperation includes a strong focus on supporting regional integration, including through its long-term support to the African Union, African Regional Economic Communities and dedicated initiatives such as the Sahel Alliance.

While centralizing political responsibility for development policy, both countries see an increasing number of line ministries getting involved in managing development cooperation projects, and a corresponding increase in various agencies and organizations involved in implementing these. The Ministry of Foreign Affairs, for instance, recently observed that 44 different agencies were involved in implementing Korean projects. For both countries—though to different degrees and with different priorities—this level of fragmentation raises questions about issues that include results reporting, the introduction and use of standard indicators, independent evaluations, consistent ODA reporting and promoting effective cooperation.

Conclusions

In the digital age, geographical proximity is no longer a requirement for cooperation and joint policy initiatives. Instead, converging norms, ideas and interests should reinforce cooperation, as cross-border cooperation remains a precondition for establishing the only path to ensure global sustainable development. This chapter has explored the case for cooperation between two countries that have made efforts to promote the 2030 Agenda, both domestically and internationally, and sought to describe how engaging in further horizontal dialogue and cooperation on shared priorities could be of mutual benefit.

Germany and Korea strongly support the 2030 Agenda, both domestically and through international cooperation, yet their policies and operations are confronted by a challenging global geopolitical and economic setting and a decline in human development across the globe. In a way, many countries are returning to a situation similar to the time of the Millennium Development Goals, when direct needs and public services were a key requirement—food security being a very evident one. The need for an additional focus on basic needs and humanitarian aid will be a reality of cooperation, also given the rising levels of inequality and the disproportionally distributed effects of climate change.

This chapter has argued that in this challenging global context there is significant scope for strengthening cooperation between Germany and Korea. Both countries face a challenging learning curve in responding to a crises-ridden world, with Germany experiencing challenges to uphold its commitment whereas Korea is urged to take a stronger stake in global development by increasing its resources and engagement. Further cooperation could complement the various partnerships and groups through which they conduct their international development cooperation.

References

Hong, M., & Izmestiev, A. (2020). *The transformation of the Republic of Korea's development cooperation*. UNDP Seoul Policy Centre.

Klingebiel, S. (2022). *Engaging with partners in the Global South in uncertain times* (IDOS Policy Brief 5/2022). German Institute of Development and Sustainability (IDOS).

Kwon, Hj. (2022). Reflection on a normative rationale for Korean ODA policy: Duty, self-regards, and obligation. In Hj. Kwon, T. Yamagata, E. Kim, & H. Kondoh (Eds.), *International development cooperation of Japan and South Korea* (pp. 23–43). Palgrave Macmillan.

Lee, D. Y., Son, J. W., Kim, Y. H., & Yoon, H. B. (2021). *Survey for public awareness in Korea on development cooperation*. Global Research Group, Office for Government Policy Coordination in Korea. https://www.odakorea.go.kr/fileDownLoad.xdo?f_id=16474780307972RUVUBS6JIAI3BK04K5LJ51V60

Ministry of Foreign Affairs. (2022). *Promoting global health sector cooperation with Bill & Melinda Gates Foundation*. Ministry of Foreign Affairs, Multilateral Development Cooperation and Humanitarian Assistance Division. https://www.mofa.go.kr/www/brd/m_4080/view.do?seq=372632&page=1

Morini, P. (2023). *DEL Dashboard—Germany October 2023*. Development Engagement Lab. https://developmentcompass.org/publications/briefs-and-reports/germany-dashboard-october-2023

OECD. (s.a.). *Compare your country: Thematic data collections*. https://www1.compareyourcountry.org/dev-coop-profiles-2021/en/1//default

Song, J., & Kim, E. M. (2022). South Korea's foreign aid as a foreign policy instrument. In Hj Kwon, T. Yamagata, E. Kim, & H. Kondoh (Eds.), *International development cooperation of Japan and South Korea* (pp. 73–101). Palgrave Macmillan.

CHAPTER 3

The Political Economy of German and Korean Sustainability Transitions

Thomas Kalinowski

Abstract Germany and the Republic of Korea (hereafter referred to as Korea) have ambitious goals for a green transformation but follow distinct paths that both have their strengths and weaknesses. Germany is more advanced in emission reduction, energy efficiency and environmental conscious behaviour, while Korea leads in investment in green infrastructure and industries. These distinct traits can be explained by path-dependent political economies. In Germany this created a market-oriented approach that adds an ecological dimension to the German "social market economy". Korea, on the other hand, follows the path of its "developmental state", which sees the ecological transformation as an opportunity to achieve industrial development and export leadership in green industries. Both strategies offer important insights for mutual learning as well as lessons for developed and developing countries alike.

T. Kalinowski (✉)
Graduate School of International Studies, Ewha Womans University, Seoul, Korea
e-mail: tkalinowski@ewha.ac.kr

S. Klingebiel et al. (eds.), *Emerging Trends in International Development and Climate Policy*,
https://doi.org/10.1007/978-3-031-65671-2_3

Keywords Green industrial policies · Sustainability transitions · Social market economy · Energy efficiency · Environment · Developing countries · Germany · Republic of Korea

Introduction

Both Germany and Korea have ambitious plans for a transition to sustainability and see themselves as role models for a green transformation. Yet their paths towards sustainability are remarkably different. Germany has ambitious plans for an *Energiewende* (energy transition) to replace both nuclear and coal with renewable energies. Internalizing environmental costs into market prices that nudge consumers to invest in energy saving and environmentally friendly products are at the centre of this market-oriented strategy. Korea, on the other hand, remains strongly tied to fossil and nuclear industries but prides itself on its ambitious green industrial policies that would transform the country into a global supplier of green technologies from batteries to electric vehicles (EVs). Market prices and incentives for environmentally friendly behaviour are not at the centre of this strategy, but the mission to establish the country and its companies as global leaders in green technology. Both strategies and the driving forces behind them are remarkably different and can be explained by the strong path dependency of their political economies. The transitions are therefore highly contextual and for that reason do not serve as easy role models. While this makes simple emulation of the policies difficult, an analysis of the different sustainability transitions provides important lessons that both of the countries concerned can learn from each other, as can other countries in the Global North and those in the Global South.

The Status of Sustainability Transition in Germany and Korea

Table 3.1 offers a brief sketch of the state of German and Korean sustainability transitions, with a focus on two of its most important elements: energy and mobility. Without any claim to be offering the entire picture, it illustrates the strengths and weaknesses of both distinct paths. While Germany has reduced its CO_2 emissions since the year 1990, Korea has increased them substantially. This can partly be explained by the fact that Korea has been in a process of economic catch-up, but the Korean economy also remains very energy intensive. Korea needs 0.129 kg of oil equivalent to produce one dollar of its GDP, while Germany needs just about half of that (Table 3.1). The Korean Nationally Determined Contributions (NDCs) emission goals under the 2015 Paris Agreement are also far less ambitious than those of Germany. Korea is also a laggard when it comes to renewable energy, as its installed wind power capacity and the market share of EVs remain small. The latter is particularly surprising because Hyundai-Kia is one of the global leaders in EV production and technology. In fact, Roland Berger and Forschungsgesellschaft Kraftfahrwesen Aachen (fka) (2021) ranks Korea number one in EV technology, with Germany coming in third place after Korea and China.

Hyundai is also by far the world's largest producer of fuel cell vehicles based on hydrogen. Even more importantly, Korea is a leader in EV battery technology, the most important component of all EVs. Three Korean companies, LG, SK and Samsung, are among the top seven of global lithium-ion battery makers and command 26% of the world market (Statista, 2023b, p. 33). More strikingly, the Korean government and

Table 3.1 Status of sustainability transition in Germany and Korea

	Germany	*Korea*
Change in CO_2 emissions 1990–2022 (%)	–33.2	+133.5
2030 NDC emission reduction targets (%)	65 (base yr. 1990)	40 (2018)
Energy intensity of GDP (in kilogramme oil equivalent per USD-PPP)	0.065	0.129
Renewable share in electricity (%)	46.2	8.05
Installed wind capacity in GW	66	1.9
EV 2022 sales share (%)	31	9.4
Public EV chargers	77,000	210,000
Fuel cell vehicle fleet (2020)	2,300	29,600
EV battery company global market share (%)	0 (Goal for EU in 2030: 30)	26
Investments in batteries up to 2030 (Euro)	1.5 bn (+3.2 bn from EU)	35 bn
Green Party votes in last parliamentary election (%)	14.8 (2021)	2.15 (2024)

Sources Enerdata (n.d.), The Korean–German Energy Partnership (n.d.), IEA50 (2023), IEEE Spectrum (2021), Visual Capitalist (2022), and Statista (2023a, 2023b)

companies are planning to invest KRW 50 trillion (EUR 35 billion) in battery research and production until 2030 (Korea JoongAng Daily, 2022, November 1). Compared to these massive investments, the German government's plan to invest EUR 1.5 billion in batteries is negligible, even when the German share of the EUR 3.2 billion of EU investments in this field are included.

Strong investments in Korea are not limited to research and development of green products but also extend to green infrastructure. Despite a low share of EVs on the street, Korea has almost three times as many public chargers as Germany (although only a minority are "fast chargers"). While Germany needs vast resources just to maintain its ageing public transport infrastructure, Korea is investing KRW 115 trillion (EUR 81 billion) in the *expansion* of rail infrastructure until 2030, prioritizing on connecting the densely populated Metropolitan Area around Seoul with the city (Yonhap, 2021, April 22). In addition to many subway line extensions, three completely new GTX high-speed commuter lines are under construction or planned, with the first line to be opened in 2024. This Korean version of the French express commuter trains (RER) will have top speeds of 180 km/h and run in tunnels 50 metres below ground. These investments meet a strong demand for public transport. Before the Corona pandemic Korean train passengers travelled 100 billion km a year. German rail passengers travelled just 2% more, despite a population that is 60% larger and a territory that is 260% bigger than South Korea's. The populations of both countries remain devoted to their cars, and in Korea it seems that cars have now become even more important as a status symbol than in Germany. At the same time, Germans travel almost 1 trillion km on the road, while Koreans drive only about 390 billion km a year (all transport data from OECD, 2023c).

The fact that Germany is such a laggard compared to Korea when it comes to investment in green industries and infrastructure, is surprising given that environmental topics play a much central role in German society and politics than in Korea. The 2021 parliamentary elections in Germany were even dubbed the "climate elections", with the Green Party winning 14.8% of the votes compared to just 2.15% for the Korean Green Party / Justice Party alliance in the 2024 parliamentary election. While in Germany strong environmental consciousness and demand for green consumption is hampered by lack of investment, in Korea investment in infrastructure leads to environmentally friendly behaviour, despite environmental topics not playing an important role in societal and political discourses.

Patterns of Environmental Transition and Green Technological Leadership

Examining these scattered facts, a pattern emerges. Germany is leading Korea when it comes to renewable energy, reduction of CO_2 emissions and energy saving. In Germany, consumers increasingly make choices that take sustainability into account and demand ambitious sustainability goals from their government. Unfortunately, green investments lag behind societal discourses. While many Germans would like to take public transport, they struggle amid a failing infrastructure. At the same time, German governments are more generous when it comes to subsidizing environmentally friendly behaviour. Consumers were eager to buy (often foreign-made) EVs with government subsidies even before German car makers belatedly decided to pivot away from combustion engines and invest in EVs. In Germany, carbon prices were introduced to nudge industries to invest in more energy efficient production, and a new "heating law" (GEG) was passed in 2023 with the goal to mobilize investments from real-estate owners into energy-efficient heating. Germany also first introduced the EUR 9 (and now the EUR 49) nationwide monthly rail ticket ("Deutschlandticket"), the huge success of which led to a rethinking of the decade-long prioritization of cars and a shift towards investment in rail modernization.

In Korea, things generally work the other way around as environmental consciousness, behaviour and consumption follow investment and government initiatives. Environmentally friendly choices evolve when supply by companies and leadership by the government is provided. Koreans take public transport not primarily out of environmental consciousness but because investment in infrastructure has made it convenient to do so. Now the city of Seoul—after investment in the rail infrastructure—is planning a version of the "Deutschlandticket" that will provide unlimited rides for KRW 65,000 (about EUR 45) a month. It is initially limited to Seoul, but the ambition is for a country-wide expansion (Hankyoreh, 2023, September 12).

Also only recently, Koreans have started buying EVs as Korean companies have developed them with support from the government. Interestingly, Korea is one of the few countries where Tesla does not lead sales in EVs. Tesla's best-selling Model 3 comes in only in eighth place, with eight of the top ten EVs made by Hyundai-Kia (Statista, 2023a). In fact, EV-only companies like Tesla were excluded from some of the government support, giving an advantage to local producers (Korea Times, 2021, January 7). It is likely that EV sales will catch up with the EV market share in Germany as more and more Hyundai–Kia models become available. At the same time, both companies and governments are heavily investing in technologies necessary for the green transition, such as batteries, semiconductors and hydrogen. The goal is first and foremost to make Korean companies green technology leaders in these fields, with the environmental transition as a secondary goal.

On the other hand, Germany follows a different strategy. Its focus is not the technological leadership of German companies but reducing prices for products needed for the sustainability transition and improving the attractiveness of the "Standort Deutschland" for private investors. The primary justification for this competition for investment are general goals such as economic growth and the creation of jobs, but not development of specific industries. In fact, industrial policies that support a specific company are seen as incompatible with the German version of neoliberalism, the "ordo-liberal" conviction that direct state interventions are bad, because they distort the market. More recently industrial policies are discussed in Germany, but not in the context of supporting the growth of certain industries and firms but to increase market competition and reduce dependence on certain trading partners, in particular Russia and China. This strategy is often referred to as "de-risking" and diversifying supply. The most prominent case recently discussed was the Intel semiconductor factory in Magdeburg, which will receive EUR 10 billion in subsidies (Der Spiegel, 2023, June 19). At the centre of this plan is not the development of a German chip industry that could emerge as a new competitor to global oligopolists such as Intel, TSMC and Samsung, but securing market supply of chips and creating high tech-jobs.

Bottom-Up Dynamics and the Environmental Movement in Germany

After this brief and admittedly incomplete comparison between the status of German and Korean sustainability transition, let us now look at some of the reasons behind the differences. A central element of the explanation is the distinctly different political economies of the transition process or, in other words, by the different political and economic driving forces behind the transition. The German transition was very much initiated from the bottom up by an environmental movement against the resistance of business and conservative political forces. This is exemplified by the rise of the German Green Party from the left-wing fringe in the early 1980s to a governing party, winning 14.8% of the vote in the 2021 parliamentary election. Slowly and gradually the green movement managed to mainstream sustainability. Today, even within conservative political parties such as the FDP and the CDU, as well as conservative newspapers such as the *Frankfurter Allgemeine Zeitung* and *Welt*, there is a certain agreement on the goal of sustainability—as long as it is done in a "market-friendly" way, i.e. as long as the state plays a facilitating and not a leading role.

The result of this mainstream consensus was the extension of the German "social market economy" by an ecological dimension. In such a social-ecological market economy the government abstains from direct interventions. It is instead characterized by a focus on market mechanisms supplemented by redistribution. In an ecological market economy, energy prices are increased through carbon trading markets or taxes. These increasing prices are then mitigated through direct subsidies to companies (such as exemption from energy taxes) and welfare spending to households, for example covering heating costs in addition to the *Bürgergeld* (basic welfare). Through the combination of mild market nudging with redistribution, resistance against the necessity of a green transition has been marginalized to political fringes, and citizens even accept one of the highest electricity prices in the world. The success of this strategy largely depends on the strong redistributive ability of the state that helps mitigate the costs of the transition. In fact, government spending as a share of GDP in Germany was 51% of GDP in 2021, much higher than the 38% redistributed in Korea (OECD, 2023a).

In Korea the redistributive capacity of the state remains limited, and the environmental movement has failed to establish an ideological hegemony. Consequently, the government finds it difficult to implement even the most modest increases in energy prices. On the contrary, the government massively subsidizes energy consumption by financing huge deficits in the state-owned energy provider KEPCO, which ran a deficit of KRW 33 trillion (EUR 23 billion) in 2022 alone (Yonhap, 2023). Due to low energy prices, and the small role that environmental topics play in public discourses, environmental consciousness and willingness to save energy remain weak.

While the environmental movement in Korea is generally well organized, it lacks agenda-setting power. Environmental NGOs focus on domestic environmental protection and not global issues such as climate change. They are quite able to prevent local projects that are environmentally problematic, and even achieved a (short-lived) moratorium on nuclear power plant constructions, but they lack the ability to set the agenda and play little role in the overall political debate. The societal discourses remain dominated by a "development narrative" in which Korea is still seen as an underdeveloped country struggling to succeed and in need of a strong government leading the way. In fact, despite the overall (average) wealth that Korea has achieved, there are—unlike in Germany—still huge parts of the society with a household income below the poverty line, particularly among the elderly. In Korea, about 40% of those aged 66 and older have an income below the poverty line (Germany 11%), i.e. less than half of the median income (OECD, 2023d). This has to do with the fact that many of the older generation have not paid into the public pension system that has only been expanded since the 1990s.

Korea also lacks a comprehensive social security system that could cushion higher energy prices for the socially weak. There is not even a social consensus that the state should support the poor at all, and welfare policies tend to be much more targeted towards certain goals, such as increasing the birth rate or supporting house ownership. The lack of a comprehensive welfare state limits the ability to compensate consumers for increasing energy prices. More generally, Koreans tend to underestimate the importance of Korea for global environmental efforts, despite its role as the seventh largest emitter of CO_2—just one place behind Germany. Air pollution is another example where public discourses underestimate Korea's role, while stressing the contribution of fine dust coming from China (Korea Herald, 2017), although most of the fine dust is actually originating in Korea (Yonhap, 2019, November 20).

The price for the environmental mainstreaming in Germany was that the mission to create a sustainable Germany was co-opted by the social-ecological market economy in which the state sees itself only as a facilitator of private initiatives. This business-friendly logic led to the German transition focusing too much on prices, regulations and incentives, while neglecting direct interventions and public investments. Industries with strong lobbying power were often able to negotiate exemptions, while households with low income and limited savings often felt overwhelmed. For them, despite the more or less generous subsidies, the increase in energy costs, the transition to EVs and the investments (or rent hikes) needed to instal energy efficient heating are a major financial burden. Ultimately, the middle class pays for the brunt of the sustainability transition, while many businesses and high-income households receive subsidies although they would have been able to instal a new heating system or purchase a new EV without them. The downside of this market-oriented strategy is that it neglects necessary public investments, and undermines the ability of the state to implement the more radical changes needed to achieve the obligations of international treaties such as the Paris Agreement. The strong public backlash against the heating law that was stirred by the conservative opposition and newspapers in 2023, often with exaggerated or false reports based on a leaked internal draft of the law, is an example that support for sustainability remains precarious even in Germany (see "Die Zeit", 2023, September 8).

The Korean Neo-Developmental State and Green Industrial Policies

The green transition in Korea evolves in a completely different way, as the government takes the lead in green industrial policies. Most German policymakers (and in particularly their economic advisors) still need to be persuaded of the positive roles of an interventionist state, while Korean governments, regardless of political leaning, have made it their mission to establish Korea as an industrial and export leader in green technology. Industrial policies here refer to government initiatives that directly support a specific domestic industry. In this sense it is different from market regulatory, macroeconomic and infrastructure policies that apply to all industries alike, as well as measures stimulating consumption of green products. A subsidy for the purchase of an EV as such is thus not an industrial policy, as it benefits not just domestic industries. In Korea, not nudging market actors towards sustainability but direct partnership with domestic businesses in developing green export industries is the goal.

The "K-battery strategy" can serve as an illustration of Korea's industrial policies. Referring to the global success of K-Pop for branding, this strategy brings together the government, research institutes and battery makers to be "the number one EV battery manufacturing country in the world by 2030" (IEA [International Energy Agency], 2022). The goal is to form an "industrial network" and a "grand alliance" that creates synergy and reduces unnecessary competition. Three of the seven largest battery producers (SK, LG and Samsung) already come from Korea, and until 2030, with government support, they will invest KRW 50 trillion (EUR 35 billion) into research and new facilities. While this government support is focused on tax incentives and support for research and development (R&D) it tends to be much more focused on developing marketable projects than on research as such. More importantly, Korea invests much more in R&D generally, spending 4.9% of its GDP, the second highest share in the OECD after Israel, with Germany trailing at just 3.1%. Of 1,000 employees in Korea 17.3 work in research, the highest in the OECD, compared to just 10.3 in Germany (OECD, 2023b).

This close cooperation between the state and a few large business groups organized by the government has often been referred to as the Korean version of a developmental state; it is credited with Korea's successful economic development from the 1960s until at least the 1990s (for an overview of the literature see Woo-Cumings, 1999). In fact, while this developmental state has been modified through various reforms, there is a strong path dependency. For example, since the 1990s Korea has refrained from outright protectionism and has preferred more subtle means to protect domestic companies from foreign competitors, while at the same time using market opening to prevent rent-seeking and force domestic companies to invest in competitiveness. The government has lost the ability to order private businesses to invest by controlling their access to capital, research and international markets. Today, the large Korean business conglomerates (*chaebol*) are multinational companies that generally do not depend on the government for mobilizing funding and research. Consequently, over time, the relationship between state and business has changed from a partnership in which the government leads into a corporatist alliance in which the state has become the junior partner of big business. This is what I have called the Korean "neo-developmental state" (for a more detailed explanation see Kalinowski,

2021). In fact, in many ways coordination between state and big business is now easier than during the times of the classic developmental state, because economic concentration has further intensified. In fact, the key players in EV manufacturing, Hyundai-Kia, and the three battery makers, LG, SK and Samsung, represent four of the five largest chaebol, which together control 50% of assets and 57% of the income of the 76 largest business groups in Korea (KFTC [Korea Fair Trade Commission], 2022, p. 9).

Chaebols are not just companies but conglomerates that consist of multiple companies in diverse business fields. SK, for example, has 165 affiliate companies ranging from oil and petrochemicals to semiconductors and telecommunication. Hyundai has 56 affiliates and Samsung 59. The advantage of this business structure is that a conglomerate can mobilize large sums for new investments within a short period of time. Despite their size and being listed on the stock market, the five largest conglomerates are controlled by their founding families through relatively small shareholdings. This central control ensures that investment priorities within the group are supported by all affiliates. In addition, non-affiliated suppliers are part of the centralized chaebol ecosystem, further adding to the centralized economic structure. This centralized business structure also allows a close cooperation with the government. In fact, when President Moon announced that "Our goal is obvious: to become the undisputed No.1 country for batteries by 2030" (Moon, 2021) the CEOs of all three battery makers were present. The ability to coordinate a whole industry with all relevant people present in a small conference room is the strength of the Korean neo-developmental state. The downsides are equally obvious: a large concentration of economic power in a few hands facilitates corruption, stifles SMEs and undermines markets and competition. In fact, the neo-developmental state is distinctively anti-market by "getting prices wrong" and limiting "wasteful competition" (Amsden, 1989), which is beneficial for companies and rapid economic growth but bad for consumers.

On the other hand, Germany finds it difficult to implement industrial policies due to institutional constraints and an ideological focus on neoliberal (or in German "ordo-liberal") market regulation. The German political economy is almost the counter-concept of the Korean. State and economy are decentralized, with economic policies split over 16 German states and an economic policy targeted at the strong economic role of SMEs ("Mittelstand"). This Mittelstand is highly specialized, competitive and innovative but lacks the ability to mobilize large amounts of capital for investment. The large number of SMEs are also difficult to coordinate, and any support for one or a few companies will necessarily have ramifications for others, particularly in times of scarce skilled labour. Politically, the situation is complicated further by the EU, which on the one hand extended the market for German products and investments but on the other hand makes industrial policies difficult. In the EU, competition and creating a level playing field, not industrial development, are seen as the guiding principles of the economy. In this context, industrial policies are suspicious as the whole purpose is that governments support domestic industrial development to gain a competitive edge over others. This does not mean that there are no industrial policies in Germany, but they are not geared towards national industrial leadership but primarily towards job creation.

Lessons for Development in a World in Transition

This chapter has looked at two very distinct paths to sustainability that both have their strengths and weaknesses. At this time, it is not possible to judge which of the two paths will be more successful as this will only become clear empirically over the years. The described distinct developments are shaped by the path dependency of distinct political economies, which makes it difficult to simply transfer policies from Germany to Korea or the other way round. Korea can adopt German policies concerning energy, or copy carbon pricing, but that does not mean that the effects or the societal acceptance for them will be the same. Similarly, Germany can copy elements of Korean industrial policy, but that would neither create the same kind of centralized coordination, alter EU scrutiny of subsidies nor overcome resistance from the ordo-liberal establishment. Of course, that does not mean that learning from each other is impossible or futile, but rather the opposite. Knowledge about alternative strategies is essential to avoid hubris as well as the naivety of attempting simple policy transplants. The art of any successful policy learning does not primarily depend on the merit of the adopted policy as such, but on how measures are adapted to the local circumstances.

Finally, when it comes to lessons for countries in the Global South, the comparison also revealed some important insights. Countries with a strong environmental movement and a capable redistributive state can consider lessons from the German path. In particular, some South American countries with strong civil societies might find such a route based on grassroots support feasible, although this would in most cases require modernization of the welfare state from a patronage system to an effective redistribution mechanism. Most countries in the Global South, however, might find the Korean path to be more accessible. Building a developmental state based on state leadership and the nurturing of a domestic capitalist class is not easy, but it arguably easier to adapt to local conditions than building strong market institutions and a strong civil society. Ultimately, the important take-home message is the there are multiple paths to sustainability, and every society must learn how to shape its own path, based on specific strengths and lessons from other countries. The path towards sustainability is not set. It is thus not important to follow a specific path but to arrive at the destination.

References

Amsden, A. H. (1989). *Asia's next giant: South Korea and late industrialization*. Oxford University Press. http://www.loc.gov/catdir/enhancements/fy0640/88036231-d.html

Berger, R., & Forschungsgesellschaft Kraftfahrwesen Aachen. (2021). *E-Mobility Index 2021*.

Caspari, L., Otto, F., Schlieben, M., Schuler, K. & Reinbold, F. (2023, September 8). Wir waren im absoluten Krisenmodus. *Die Zeit*. https://www.zeit.de/politik/deutschland/2023-09/gebaeudeenergiegesetz-heizungsgesetz-bundestag-ampel-koalition. Accessed 23 January 2024.

Da-sol, K. (2017, January 3). 70% of Korea's fine dust particles come from China: Study. *The Korea Herald*. https://www.koreaherald.com/view.php?ud=20170103000745. Accessed 23 January 2024.

Enerdata. (n.d.). *World energy & climate statistics—Yearbook 2023*. Enerdata. https://yearbook.enerdata.net/total-energy/world-energy-intensity-gdp-data.html. Accessed 23 January 2024.

IEA (International Energy Agency). (2022). *Global EV Outlook*.

IEA50. (2023). *Global EV data explorer*. https://www.iea.org/data-and-statistics/data-tools/global-ev-data-explorer. Accessed 23 October 2023.

IEEE Spectrum. (2021). *The top 10 EV battery markers*. https://spectrum.ieee.org/the-top-10-ev-battery-makers. Accessed 23 October 2023.

Ji-min, S. (2023, September 12). Seoul to offer unlimited public transit pass for $49 per month starting in 2024. *The Hankyoreh*. https://english.hani.co.kr/arti/english_edition/e_national/1108220.html

Kalinowski, T. (2021). The politics of climate change in a neo-developmental state: The case of South Korea. *International Political Science Review, 42*(1). https://doi.org/10.1177/0192512120924741

KFTC (Korea Fair Trade Commission). (2022). *Large business groups 2022.*

Kim, B. (2021a, January 7). Tesla protests against Korea's green car incentive program. *Korean Times*. https://www.koreatimes.co.kr/www/tech/2023/10/129_302119.html. Accessed 23 January 2024.

Kim, E-J. (2021b, April 22). S. Korea to invest 114 tln won by 2039 to expand railway network. *Yonhap News Agency*. https://en.yna.co.kr/view/AEN20210422003100320

Lee, H. (2022, November 1). Big battery alliance brings government and companies together. *Korea JoongAng Daily*. https://koreajoongangdaily.joins.com/2022/11/01/business/industry/Secondary-battery-rechargeable-battery-IRA/20221101184802456.html. Accessed 23 January 2024.

Moon, J.-i. (2021). *Remarks by President Moon Jae-in at K-Battery development strategy presentation*. https://www.korea.net/Government/Briefing-Room/Presidential-Speeches/view?articleId=200817

OECD. (2023a). *General government spending (indicator)*. https://data.oecd.org/gga/general-government-spending.htm. Accessed 23 October 2023.

OECD. (2023b). *Gross domestic spending on R&D (indicator)*. https://data.oecd.org/rd/gross-domestic-spending-on-r-d.htm. Accessed 23 October 2023.

OECD. (2023c). *Passenger transport (indicator)*. https://data.oecd.org. Accessed 23 October 2023.

OECD. (2023d). *Poverty rate (indicator)*. https://data.oecd.org. Accessed 23 October 2023.

Statista. (2023a). *Change in carbon dioxide emissions in selected countries worldwide from 1990 to 2022*. https://www.statista.com/statistics/270500/percentage-change-in-co2-emissions-in-selected-countries/. Accessed 23 October 2023.

Statista. (2023b). *Volume of fuel cell electric vehicle (FCEV) stock in the Asia-Pacific region in 2020, by country and type*. https://www.statista.com/statistics/1246477/apac-fcev-stock-volume-by-country-and-type/. Accessed 23 October 2023.

The Korean–German Energy Partnership. (n.d.). https://www.energypartnership-korea.org/home/. Accessed 23 January 2024.

Traufetter, G. (2023, June 19). *Habeck stellt weitere drei Milliarden Euro bereit für Intel-Chipfabrik in Magdeburg*. Der Spiegel. https://www.spiegel.de/wirtschaft/unternehmen/intel-chipfabrik-in-magdeburg-robert-habeck-stellt-weitere-drei-milliarden-euro-aus-klimafonds-bereit-a-3603cf77-0ae3-4cee-8291-d606ff2bab4b. Accessed 23 January 2024.

Visual Capitalist. (2022). *The top 10 EV battery manufacturers in 2022*. https://www.visualcapitalist.com/the-top-10-ev-battery-manufacturers-in-2022/. Accessed 23 October 2023.

Woo-Cumings, M. (Ed.) (1999). *The developmental state*. Cornell University Press.

CHAPTER 4

Positions of Established and Emerging Powers Towards Climate Finance: The Cases of Germany and Korea

R. Melis Baydag

Abstract Climate finance is an increasingly important issue for international cooperation of established and emerging powers as well as their claims of leadership in the global green energy transition. This chapter explores the underpinnings of the positions of Germany and South Korea towards international climate finance from the perspective of ideational and material interest-driven domestic political dynamics.

Keywords Climate finance · Green energy transition · Domestic politics · Germany · South Korea

R. M. Baydag (✉)
German Institute of Development and Sustainability (IDOS), Bonn, Germany
e-mail: melis.baydag@idos-research.de

S. Klingebiel et al. (eds.), *Emerging Trends in International Development and Climate Policy*,
https://doi.org/10.1007/978-3-031-65671-2_4

Introduction

Climate finance is an increasingly important issue for international cooperation of established actors such as Germany and emerging actors such as the Republic of Korea (hereafter referred to as Korea) as well as their claims of global leadership in the green energy transition. Climate politics, on the one hand, involves national policies on green energy transformation to a great extent and is therefore "motivated by domestic economic priorities, the global pressure for competitiveness, and the desire to secure better positions in global production and trade networks" (Allan et al., 2021, p. 4). On the other hand, governance of climate requires cooperation, in which highly industrialized developed countries are expected to take responsibility, for example, for addressing the challenges faced by vulnerable developing countries.

In this chapter, I explore the domestic and international linkages in the climate politics of established and emerging powers, drawing on the cases of Germany and Korea. The motivations behind the stances of the governments of Germany and Korea on international climate finance have aligned in terms of supporting global green energy transition and aiding developing countries in climate change efforts. Despite this convergence, the driving forces behind these positions differ. The German government blends ideational and material interests-driven aspects in its position, emphasizing collective responsibility along with a strong emphasis on renewable energy and nuclear phase-out; whereas the Korean government takes an economically driven approach that, alongside renewables, focuses on cooperation in nuclear energy that benefits its domestic sectors. Recognizing these differences highlights the need to understand domestic–international connections in climate finance and identify variations in national-level climate policies.

Emerging and Established Powers in Climate Cooperation

The main debates in international efforts to mitigate climate change centre on two issues: The first concerns nationally determined contributions (NDCs), such as strategies to reduce CO_2 emissions or to shift energy supplies to sustainable energy sources. The second is about compensating, through climate finance, for the damage faced by vulnerable developing countries. The latter is particularly important for determining the global responsibilities in climate cooperation.

On matters of climate governance, both established and emerging power positions seek to find a balance between economic growth and climate change mitigation. This has been a key concern in particular for emerging powers. On the one hand, they have been reluctant to make environmental protection commitments that could hinder their economic growth potential, while, on the other, they have taken the position that highly industrialized countries have historical responsibilities for climate change and should allocate *more* resources for climate finance (Destradi & Jakobeit, 2015). Established powers, such as European states, whose emissions from their industrialization processes have historically exacerbated climate change, emphasize the burden-sharing purposes in their international cooperation on climate matters. In their aid strategies, however, they tend to combine assisting developing countries (and thus addressing their needs) with medium- and long-term interest-driven strategies regarding the provision of global public goods or their export interests (Baydag & Klingebiel, 2023). Besides economic concerns, challenges stemming from European and global crises, such as Russia's war in Ukraine or the Covid-19 pandemic, have caused substantial shifts in state preferences towards more nation-centred and security-oriented policies. The importance of, or priority given to, climate mitigation has reduced vis-à-vis the concerns for securing one's energy supply and fighting against rising energy prices (Feist & Geden, 2023).

In light of these issues, the variations in the positions of established and emerging powers in international climate cooperation can be observed during the negotiations at the United Nations Framework Convention on Climate Change (UNFCCC) Conference of the Parties (COP). The main debates at COP27 in 2022, for instance, concentrated on creating a dedicated multilateral fund for climate finance and the question of who should take (more) responsibility for financing poorer countries to help them mitigate the damage caused by climate change, i.e. the loss and damage fund. The problem was mainly with the UNFCCC's developing country categorization, which has not been updated since the 1992 Climate Convention. This raised the issue of free riders, as it includes a long list of countries ranging from particularly climate-vulnerable ones (e.g. small island states) to emerging economies that are now among the largest CO_2 emitters (e.g. China). As a result, negotiations on creating the fund provoked a strong reaction from European states such as Germany. They oppose the categorization of emerging economies such as China, Korea and Singapore—which have become significant emitters due to their rapid industrial growth—as developing countries on the grounds that it prevents climate finance from benefiting countries that need it most (The Economist, 2022). Furthermore, the European position has also emphasized the responsibilities of emerging economies such as China and Gulf petrostates in financing poorer countries (Harvey, 2023). Similarly, at COP28 in 2023, the reluctance of oil-producing countries led to a consensus only on a *transition away* from fossil fuels towards renewable energies rather than a more stringent phase-out plan. Furthermore, during COP28, 22 countries, including the US, some European countries such as the UK and France, as well as emerging economies such as Korea pledged to increase their nuclear energy capacity to help achieve rapid decarbonization by 2050 (Gross, 2023). On nuclear power, Germany singles itself out from other established powers because of having finalized its nuclear phase-out in 2023.

The examples demonstrate that issue-specific governmental positions in climate negotiations go beyond the categorizations of positions based on established and emerging powers, but rather stem from their national preferences. While certain divergences in governmental positions that broadly define these categories have persisted (e.g. controversies on who should take more responsibility for the multilateral climate finance), convergences in positions can also be observed (e.g. promoting nuclear energy for decarbonization). Furthermore, they also diverged from their respective groups in certain aspects (e.g. Germany's non-nuclear commitments vis-à-vis other established states).

Ideational and material interest-driven motivations have somewhat converged in the positions of the governments of Germany and Korea towards international climate finance, for example, towards the necessity of a global green energy transition and responsibility in financing developing countries in their efforts to tackle climate change. Although this might imply a lessening of differentiations in terms of positions among the established and emerging group of actors, the motivations as drivers of these preferences have nevertheless differed significantly. Accordingly, the German government has taken a mixture of ideational and material interest-driven positions in assisting developing countries that both emphasized collective action of advanced and emerging economies and pursued the domestic interests of the renewable sectors in green energy transition. The Korean positions followed a more pragmatic economic interest-driven approach, giving more weight to nuclear energy as an important source of clean energy while pointing to energy security and sector interests, in addition to renewable energy. This calls for the importance of domestic–international linkages in climate finance and the identification of the main differences in national-level climate policies.

International Climate Finance and Domestic Politics

Broadly speaking, my starting point is that international commitments hinge on the dynamics of domestic politics. Due to limitations imposed by domestic politics, the likelihood of establishing a consensus in climate negotiations significantly depends on the level of support from the domestic public and elites (Keohane & Oppenheimer, 2016). Governments of both established and emerging powers are expected to align their national climate targets with international commitments. In consequence, while national strategies shape commitments of states towards international climate finance, discrepancies between those two may hinder multilateralism (Etzioni, 2018).

The main argument in this paper lies on international political economy (IPE) approaches concurring on two key points concerning domestic preference formation (Katzenstein, 1977; Milner, 1997; Moravcsik, 1997). First, grounded in the concept of democratic representation, these approaches assume government responsiveness, asserting that governing politicians tend to align their policies with voter preferences in order to retain office. However, this responsiveness is not absolute, as it is limited by factors such as interest-group influence and bureaucratic constraints. The state as a representative institution is subject to constant capture and reconstruction by social coalitions. Governments incorporate dominant societal preferences into their policies to appeal to a crucial segment of society. In essence, state preferences reflect the interpretations of powerful domestic groups on security, welfare and sovereignty. Second, IPE approaches challenge the assumption that states inherently prioritize their interests, particularly those related to power and security, which are often considered fixed or uniform (Milner, 1997; Moravcsik, 1997). This critique extends to power-centric realist perspectives and rule-based institutionalism, which predominantly emphasize systemic factors like power distribution or the role of international institutions, and overlook the impact of domestic elements on shaping the policy preferences of nation-states and, consequently, international outcomes. As such, a domestic politics perspective offers a more nuanced understanding of state preferences by highlighting the intricate dynamics of domestic politics.

From this domestic politics perspective, international climate finance strategies of German and Korean governments are argued to follow their national-level policies. In other words, the roles of demands of domestic sector groups and ideational expectations in the society in shaping the German and Korean green energy transition—as well as possible interplay among these domestic factors in policy processes (Schirm, 2020)—is decisive for the international commitments of the two governments. First, climate policy, or "policy change" through energy transition (Hochstetler, 2020), has distributional consequences in domestic politics due to several industrial strategies that concern sectors such as those in conventional and renewable energy. In addition, governments want to secure the energy supply for their domestic industries. Second, green industrial policies have distributive implications for voters (Allan et al., 2021) and therefore touch upon "path-dependent, value-based societal expectations" and "general societal interests" (Schirm, 2020), creating dichotomies, such as expectations from the government in environmental protection vis-à-vis economic growth. Furthermore, these policies are also expected to significantly follow domestic institutions and socio-economic structures that inform decision-making (Hochstetler, 2020; Kalinowski, 2020). As such, certain groups and individuals in the society, who are likely to be potential beneficiaries, will support the government's policies on climate mitigation, whereas some others will resist it. Both governments would not risk their term in office and therefore avoid climate policies that run counter to the dominant expectations in the society.

The German and Korean governmental positions on international climate cooperation in green energy transition reflect domestic political dynamics. In the next section, I briefly examine the role of domestic ideas in their commitments to solidarity with climate-vulnerable countries and the impact of nuclear power strategies on their support for green energy transition cooperation as illustrative cases. Due to the constraints on the length of the chapter, a comprehensive analysis of domestic preference formation is reserved for future work. I look at the divergences from the perspective of their domestic strategies, which are assumed to reflect certain value-orientated perceptions and/or material economic interests of groups and individuals.

German and Korean Positions Towards International Climate Finance

In international climate finance, the positions of German and Korean governments are in line with their national strategies on green energy transition. These seem to converge in some ways (e.g. investing in hydrogen energy and financing projects in developing and emerging countries), yet follow opposite directions in significant aspects. One of those stems from the ideational differences in terms of how the government defines its global responsibilities in climate governance. German governmental commitments focus on *solidarity* with the most vulnerable developing countries, whereas the Korean position concentrates more on the *cooperation* aspect. Concerning the contributions of emerging economies to the loss and damage fund, as debated in the COP27—which closely concerns Korea—the Yoon administration has not taken an explicit position but rather adopted a rhetoric on assisting climate-vulnerable countries as well as increasing green official development assistance (ODA) to them. This seems to have contradicted Korea's official position that emphasized Korea's ameliorated status as an advanced country since its membership to OECD Development Assistance Committee in 2010. The German governmental position, on the other hand, emphasized "the very special responsibilities" of industrialized countries, as well as of those emerging economies "among the biggest emitters today" in climate action (Scholz, 2023). In addition, the case of Germany also demonstrates certain shifts in how established powers define their role in international climate cooperation. The government emphasized Germany's efforts as a "bridge-builder" between industrialized and developing countries (German Federal Ministry for Economic Cooperation and Development, no date)—a so-called "middle power" position that has long dominated the narratives of the governments of middle-sized emerging powers such as Korea and Turkey (Baydag, 2021; Cooper & Schulz, 2023). This suggests that certain ideational dimensions in the cooperation approaches of emerging powers with developing countries are no longer unique to them. Stressing Germany's efforts for solidarity with developing countries, the speech of the German Development Minister stating, "The new fund for climate-related loss and damage within the official UN climate regime shows that we have managed to build bridges between industrialized and developing countries [...]", is illustrative in this respect (German Federal Ministry for Economic Cooperation and Development, no date).

Strong public support for international efforts for climate change mitigation can be observed in the domestic politics of both countries. The majority of Germans (58%) and Koreans (68%) believe that "actions taken by the international community will significantly reduce the effects of global climate change" (Pew Research Center, 2021). In climate negotiations, sharing responsibilities among advanced and emerging economies in providing for the climate-vulnerable developing countries was more pronounced in the German position in climate negotiations in the creation of the loss and damage fund, whereas the Korean government was broadly reluctant to share the responsibility. In line with the official German position, approximately 70% of Germans think "all countries should work together and share the responsibility of tackling climate change" (YouGov, 2023). When path-dependent domestic ideas are considered, societal expectations on *collective solidarity* vis-à-vis *individual responsibility* explains differences in the positions. For instance, the data from World Values Survey indicates that more Germans (45%) than Koreans (21%) think, "incomes should be made more equal" vis-à-vis "greater incentives for individual effort" (Haerpfer et al., 2022).

Another divergence stems from what *clean* entails in the energy transition policies of both governments and their climate cooperation for this purpose. The German governmental position in climate negotiations emphasized "sustainable, socially just, global energy transition and the decarbonization of industry" (German Federal Ministry for Economic Cooperation and Development, no date). As stated by the German Foreign Minister, it must be recognized that "the vast majority of countries around the world are committed to a future with solar and wind power, not oil and coal" (German Federal Ministry for Economic Cooperation and Development, no date). The German position excludes nuclear energy in the clean energy mix, while expanding solar and wind. The Korean climate cooperation, in contrast, significantly includes nuclear power (along with renewables) as providing clean, pragmatic and secure solutions in assisting countries that seek to reduce greenhouse gas emissions and sustain energy security (Lee, 2023). As President Yoon stated,

> Korea will not only harness renewable energy but also extensively employ high-efficiency carbon-free energy (CFE), such as nuclear power and hydrogen, as a realistic measure to hasten our pursuit of carbon neutrality. We also plan to share these energy sources with countries vulnerable to climate change, ensuring they too can benefit. (Yoon, 2023)

To this end, President Yoon announced that "Korea will launch a 'Carbon Free Alliance', an open platform that anyone in the world can join to promote the adoption of carbon-free energy" (Yoon, 2023). This platform obviously includes a significant portion of nuclear energy cooperation to be carried out also with industrialized countries, and is considered to ensure being able to meet sector-specific targets and international pledges in the green transition (Ministry of Environment of the Republic of Korea, 2022).

The German policy on the green energy transition can be partly explained by a strong public opposition to nuclear energy dating back to the 1970s, based on concerns for the dangers it poses. In 2023, the German government completed the nuclear phase-out, which was legally adopted in 2011 with a broad consensus in the domestic politics (Quitzow & Thielges, 2022). The phase-out of nuclear power, as well as expansion in renewable energy in order to generate 80% of the country's electricity by 2030, was justified by the government as "safer", given the uncontrollable risks of nuclear power (German Federal Ministry for the Environment Nature Conservation Nuclear Safety & Consumer Protection, 2022). However, as the German strategy of transition to 100% renewables still has a way to go, the alternatives are not necessarily sustainable or environmentally friendly. After the start of the Russian war on Ukraine and the resulting reduced gas flows from Russia, Germany had to reactivate coal power plants (Connolly, 2022). Its strict policy on renewables and environmental protection were therefore suspended when domestic industry interests were at stake. The crisis has, nevertheless, not led to a turning back to nuclear power, as in the case of Korea, which also suggests the persistence of anti-nuclear ideas in energy policymaking.

In Korean domestic politics, interests seem to be more prevalent in Korea's climate cooperation. For instance, along with distributing renewable energy, hydrogen and other such zero-carbon energy sources, the government increased Korea's nuclear power generation target in 2023 and abandoned the nuclear phase-out plan of the previous government due to energy security (Korean Ministry of Trade Industry & Energy,

2023). The Korean strategy mainly focused on reducing the country's energy dependence on fossil fuels by increasing the share of nuclear power in the power mix to at least 30% by 2030 (Korean Ministry of Trade Industry & Energy, 2022). In this respect, the government follows a pragmatic approach, which rests on the idea that "carbon neutrality must be accompanied by innovations and technological developments in the environment-friendly and new and renewable energy sectors because it must not become a burden for our industries", as articulated in President Yoon's statements (The Korea Times, 2022). The government emphasized the discrepancy between following a national-level climate policy based on a nuclear phase-out plan and Korean international cooperation, which heavily invests in nuclear power plant infrastructure projects overseas. The shifts in energy policy after a governmental change evidenced the persistence of the ideas of "economic developmentalism" in the process of determining the energy mix, despite public opposition to nuclear power (Cho et al., 2023; Chung & Kim, 2018). As the examples above show, while both Germany and Korea share the common goal of supporting the global transition to green energy and financing developing countries in international climate policy, the motivations behind their stances differ significantly. The explorative cases have highlighted the need for a comprehensive understanding, both conceptually and empirically, of the linkages between the national and international spheres in governmental preference formation.

Conclusion

In this chapter, I examined the preferences of established and emerging powers, using the examples of Germany and Korea, emphasizing that the diverging domestic forces shaping the green energy transition strategies of German and Korean governments explain variations in their position towards international climate finance. Ideational motivations in international climate cooperation reflect value-based domestic ideas, while the role of nuclear energy in the global green energy transition is in line with national-level priorities shaped by diverse domestic ideas and economic interests. The case studies underscore the substantial impact of national strategies on international climate finance. While some differences align with existing categorizations in the literature on established and emerging countries, a nuanced understanding of their international cooperation in global climate governance emerges when viewed through the lens of domestic politics.

References

Allan, B., Lewis, J. I., & Oatley, T. (2021). Green industrial policy and the global transformation of climate politics. *Global Environmental Politics, 21*(4), 1–19. https://doi.org/10.1162/glep_a_00640

Baydag, R. M., et al. (2021). Middle powers in international development cooperation: Assessing the roles of South Korea and Turkey. In S. Chaturvedi (Ed.), *The Palgrave handbook of development cooperation for achieving the 2030 agenda: Contested collaboration* (pp. 435–449). Palgrave Macmillan.

Baydag, R. M., & Klingebiel, S. (2023). Partner country selection between development narratives and self-interests: A new method for analysing complex donor approaches. *Review of Development Economics, 27*(2), 1199–1223.

Cho, B. K., Chung, J. B., & Song, C. K. (2023). National climate change governance and lock-in: Insights from Korea's conservative and liberal governments' committees. *Energy Strategy Reviews, 50*, 2211–2467. https://doi.org/10.1016/j.esr.2023.101238

Chung, J. B., & Kim, E. S. (2018). Public perception of energy transition in Korea: Nuclear power, climate change, and party preference. *Energy Policy, 116*, 137–144. https://doi.org/10.1016/j.enpol.2018.02.007

Connolly, K. (2022). Germany to reactivate coal power plants as Russia curbs gas flow. *The Guardian*. https://www.theguardian.com/world/2022/jul/08/germany-reactivate-coal-power-plants-russia-curbs-gas-flow. Accessed 28 November 2023.

Cooper, A. F., & Schulz, C. A. (2023). How secondary states can take advantage of networks in world politics: The case of bridges and hubs. *Globalizations, 20*(7), 1083–1101. https://doi.org/10.1080/14747731.2023.2190701

Destradi, S., & Jakobeit, C. (2015). Global governance debates and dilemmas: Emerging powers' perspectives and roles in global trade and climate governance. *Strategic Analysis, 39*(1), 60–72. https://doi.org/10.1080/09700161.2014.980538

Etzioni, A. (2018). The rising (more) nation-centered system. *Fletcher Forum of World Affairs, 42*(8), 29–54.

Feist, M., & Geden, O. (2023). *Climate negotiations in times of multiple crises: Credibility and trust in international climate politics after COP 27* (No. 10/2023). SWP Comment. https://doi.org/10.18449/2023C10

German Federal Ministry for Economic Cooperation and Development. (no date). *World climate conference: Team Germany on the conclusion of COP27* (press release). https://www.bmz.de/en/news/press-releases/team-germany-on-the-conclusion-of-cop27-129028. Accessed 28 November 2023.

German Federal Ministry for the Environment Nature Conservation Nuclear Safety and Consumer Protection. (2022). *Germany brings era of nuclear power to an end* (press release). https://www.bmuv.de/en/pressrelease/germany-brings-era-of-nuclear-power-to-an-end. Accessed 28 November 2023.

Gross, J. (2023, December 2). 22 countries pledge to triple nuclear capacity in push to cut fossil fuels. *New York Times*. https://www.nytimes.com/2023/12/02/climate/cop28-nuclear-power.html. Accessed 5 January 2024.

Haerpfer, C., Inglehart, R., Moreno, A., Welzel, C., Kizilova, K., Diez-Medrano, J., Lagos, M., Norris, P., Ponarin, E., & Puranen, B. (2022). *World values survey: Round seven-country-pooled datafile version 4.0*. JD Systems Institute. https://doi.org/10.14281/18241.20

Harvey, F. (2023). EU climate chief: China must help fund rescue of poorer nations hit by disaster. *The Guardian*. https://www.theguardian.com/environment/2023/nov/26/eu-climate-chief-china-fund-rescue-poorer-nations-cop28. Accessed 26 November 2023.

Hochstetler, K. (2020). Political economies of energy transition: Wind and solar power in Brazil and South Africa. *Cambridge University Press*. https://doi.org/10.1017/9781108920353

Kalinowski, T. (2020). The politics of climate change in a neo-developmental state: The case of South Korea. *International Political Science Review, 42*(1), 48–63. https://doi.org/10.1177/0192512120924741

Katzenstein, P. J. (1977). Introduction: Domestic and international forces and strategies of foreign economic policy. *International Organization, 31*(4), 587–606. https://doi.org/10.1017/S0020818300018622

Keohane, R. O., & Oppenheimer, M. (2016). Paris: Beyond the climate dead end through pledge and review? *Politics and Governance, 4*(3), 142–151. https://doi.org/10.17645/pag.v4i3.634

Korean Ministry of Environment. (2022). *The Minister of Environment made a policy briefing to the President*. https://m.me.go.kr/eng/web/board/read.do?pagerOffset=210&maxPageItems=10&maxIndexPages=10&searchKey=&searchValue=&menuId=461&orgCd=&boardId=1538750&boardMasterId=522&boardCategoryId=&decorator. Accessed 23 November 2023.

Korean Ministry of Trade Industry and Energy. (2022). *Korea's new energy policies are announced*. https://english.motie.go.kr/en/pc/pressreleases/bbs/bbsView.do?bbs_cd_n=2&bbs_seq_n=1008. Accessed 17 November 2023.

Korean Ministry of Trade Industry and Energy. (2023). *MOTIE to develop 11th electric power supply basic plan*. https://english.motie.go.kr/en/pc/pressreleases/bbs/bbsView.do?bbs_cd_n=2&bbs_seq_n=1363. Accessed 17 November 2023.

Lee, H. (2023). *Yoon pledges additional US$300 mln to Green Climate Fund at G20 session*. Yonhap News Agency. https://en.yna.co.kr/view/AEN20230909001100315. Accessed 26 November 2023.

Milner, H. V. (1997). Interests, institutions, and information: Domestic politics and international relations. *Princeton University Press*. https://doi.org/10.2307/j.ctv10vm16k

Moravcsik, A. (1997). Taking preferences seriously: A liberal theory of international politics. *International Organization*, 513–553. https://doi.org/10.1162/002081897550447

Quitzow, R., & Thielges, S. (2022). The German energy transition as soft power. *Review of International Political Economy, 29*(2), 598–623. https://doi.org/10.1080/09692290.2020.1813190

Pew Research Center. (2021). *In response to climate change, citizens in advanced economies are willing to alter how they live and work.* https://www.pewresearch.org/global/2021/09/14/in-response-to-climate-change-citizens-in-advanced-economies-are-willing-to-alter-how-they-live-and-work/. Accessed 8 January 2024.

Schirm, S. A. (2020). Refining domestic politics theories of IPE: A societal approach to governmental preferences. *Politics, 40*(4), 396–412. https://doi.org/10.1177/0263395719896980

Scholz, O. (2023). *Speech at the 78th General Debate of the United Nations General Assembly*. United Nations General Assembly. https://gadebate.un.org/en/78/germany. Accessed 28 November 2023.

The Economist. (2022). *Should rich countries pay for climate damage in poor ones?* https://www.economist.com/international/2022/11/20/a-new-un-fund-for-loss-and-damage-emerges-from-cop27. Accessed 16 November 2023.

The Korea Times. (2022). *Yoon takes swipe at former gov't over carbon reduction goal*. https://www.koreatimes.co.kr/www/nation/2022/10/113_338625.html. Accessed 25 November 2023.

Yoon, S. (2023). *Speech at the 78th General Debate of the United Nations General Assembly*. United Nations General Assembly. https://gadebate.un.org/en/78/republic-korea. Accessed 26 November 2023.

YouGov. (2023). *European attitudes towards climate change*. https://yougov.co.uk/topics/yougov-cambridge/home(popup:search/climate%20change. Accessed 8 January 2024.

CHAPTER 5

Realizing the Women, Peace and Security Agenda Through Foreign Aid: A Comparative Analysis of Korea and Germany

Min Joung Park

Abstract The Women, Peace and Security (WPS) agenda has gained significant traction globally as a framework to address the disproportionate impact of conflict on women and promote their active participation in peace processes. In recent years, donor countries have expanded their efforts to contribute to the implementation of the WPS agenda through their development assistance. This chapter explores how Germany and the Republic of Korea (hereafter referred to as Korea) have responded to the current trend of integrating the WPS agenda into development cooperation by analysing their National Action Plans (NAPs) on implementing the UN Security Council Resolution 1325 on women, peace and Security.

M. J. Park (✉)
Sookmyung Women's University, Seoul, Republic of Korea
e-mail: mjparkfor@gmail.com

S. Klingebiel et al. (eds.), *Emerging Trends in International Development and Climate Policy*,
https://doi.org/10.1007/978-3-031-65671-2_5

Keywords Resolution 1325 · Development cooperation · Germany · South Korea

Introduction

Since the unanimous adoption of United Nations Security Council Resolution (SCR) 1325 in October 2000, global efforts to promote and implement the Women, Peace and Security (WPS) agenda have been ongoing. The resolution marked a pivotal moment by acknowledging the disproportionate impact of armed conflict on women and emphasizing the need for their inclusion in all stages of peace processes. Subsequent UN resolutions[1] have further expanded the WPS agenda and solidified it as a cornerstone of global efforts for sustainable peace. Parallel to this UN engagement, donor countries, especially the Organisation for Economic Co-operation and Development (OECD) Development Assistance Committee (DAC) member countries, have increased their efforts to contribute to the implementation of the WPS agenda through their development assistance (OECD, 2020).

Germany and South Korea have participated in the diffusion of the WPS agenda through the Group of Friends of Women, Peace and Security (WPS), an informal network of 66 Member States and the European Union, established in 2001 under the active leadership of Canada. As a non-permanent member of the UN Security Council for the 2019–2020 term, and through its role within the European Union (EU) during its presidency, Germany led the efforts to support a comprehensive approach to the implementation of SCR 1325 and the adoption of the follow-up resolutions (Popovic, 2020). During Germany's Presidency in April 2019, Resolution 2467 was successfully adopted, calling for victims of sexual violence to be supported and perpetrators to be called to account (Birkenkötter, 2021; Federal Foreign Office, 2021; Fröhlich, 2023). South Korea, which will serve as one of the UN Security Council

[1] The follow-up resolutions of UN SCR 1325 are UN Security Council Resolution 1820 of 19 June 2008, Resolution 1888 of 30 Sep. 2009, Resolution 1889 of 30 Sep. 2010, Resolution 1960 of 16 Dec. 2010, Resolution 2106 of 24 June 2013, Resolution 2122 of 18 Oct. 2013, Resolution 2242 of 13 Oct. 2015, Resolution 2467 of 23 Apr. 2019 and Resolution 2493 of 29 Oct. 2019.

members in 2024 and 2025, identifies the WPS agenda as one of four primary areas of concern on which South Korea will lead discussions at the Council.

At the national level, Germany and South Korea have adopted their National Action Plans (NAPs) on implementing SCR 1325 using a whole-of-government approach, and development cooperation ministries and agencies have participated in implementing these NAPs. Their engagements have further increased since both countries introduced their own initiatives, such as the Action with Women and Peace Initiative in South Korea in 2018 and the Feminist Foreign Policy and the Feminist Development Policy of Germany since 2023.

This chapter explores how Germany and South Korea have responded to the recent wave of integrating the WPS agenda into development cooperation over the past decade by analysing development cooperation components in their NAPs on implementing SCR 1325, in force for the periods of 2021–2024 and 2021–2023, respectively.

Implementation of the WPS Agenda at a National Level

The concept of gender equality in peace and security was rarely incorporated in the narrative of the Security Council before the first debate on "women, peace and security" that took place in 2000 (Swaine, 2009). Such inception of the WPS agenda at the Security Council is attributed to the influence of international women's rights organizations as "norm-entrepreneurs" (Park, 2021). These groups have led the formation of international norms on peace and security from a feminist perspective by bringing to the public attention the systemic sexual crimes against women that occurred in armed conflicts in the 1990s, e.g. in Kosovo, the former Yugoslavia, Liberia, Rwanda and Sierra Leone, and by advocating for the adoption of such norms at key international gatherings, e.g. the 1993 World Conference on Human Rights in Vienna and the 1995 World Conference on Women in Beijing.

The resulting resolution from the debate, SCR 1325, has formally placed the issue of gender equality within the remit of efforts to address issues of conflict and peace, laying out four central engagement pillars: prevention, participation, protection and relief and recovery (George & Shepherd, 2016; Tryggestad, 2009). The resolution emphasizes the need to integrate gendered and inclusive approaches to sustainable peace and development while highlighting the continued targeting of women for egregious abuse in conflict situations (Popovic, 2020).

Efforts to implement SCR 1325 were accelerated when Kofi Annan, the then UN Secretary-General, asked member states to elaborate NAPs on implementing SCR 1325 in 2004 (Barrow, 2016; Jung & Tsujisaka, 2019). Since the first adoption by Denmark in 2005, NAPs have been used as a significant policy instrument to advance the implementation of the WPS agenda at the national level. NAPs set out the governments' commitments and priorities for the WPS agenda, present the human, technical and financial resources necessary to implement their plans, and have been in operation for five time periods over the past 20 years, as shown in Table 5.1. As of July 2023, 107 member states, representing 55% of the UN member states, including 28 OECD DAC members (not including Greece and Hungary), had adopted a NAP (Women's International League for Peace and Freedom, 2023). Although many countries have yet to publish their follow-up plans since establishing their first NAP, Germany and South Korea have continued to develop and implement their NAPs since 2013 and 2014, respectively.

These national efforts to implement SCR 1325 have been primarily through foreign and security policies (George & Shepherd, 2016; Muehlenhoff, 2022; Shepherd, 2016). For most donor countries, their NAPs have been developed with a focus on supporting fragile and conflict-affected states through development cooperation, recognizing that the objectives set out in SCR 1325 and subsequent resolutions are most relevant to ministries and agencies responsible for development cooperation (Popovic, 2020). As a result, bilateral ODA from DAC members focused on gender equality in fragile contexts has considerably increased, from USD 2.6 billion per year in 2002/03 to USD 10.3 billion in 2012/13 and USD 20.5 billion in 2020/2021 (OECD CRS, 2023).

Table 5.1 Global diffusion of National Action Plans (NAPs) for the implementation of UN SCR 1325

Time periods	*OECD DAC Members adopting NAPs*	*Non-OECD DAC Members adopting NAPS*
2004–2008 First movers	Denmark (2005), Norway (2006), Sweden (2006), UK (2006), Switzerland (2006), Netherlands (2007), Spain (2007), Austria (2007), Iceland (2008), Finland (2008), European Union (2008)	Côte d'Ivoire (2007), Uganda (2008)
2009–2011 SCR 1325 10-year anniversary effect	Belgium (2009), Portugal (2009), France (2010), Italy (2010), Canada (2010), Ireland (2011), US (2011)	Rwanda (2009), Guinea (2009), Liberia (2009), Chile (2009), DR Congo (2010), Bosnia and Herzegovina (2010), Serbia (2010), Sierra Leone (2010), Guinea-Bissau (2010), Philippines (2010), Slovenia (2010),[2] Croatia (2011), Georgia (2011), Burundi (2011), Nepal (2011), Senegal (2011)
2012–2015 Towards 15-year anniversary	Australia (2012), Germany (2013), Korea (2014), New Zealand (2015), Japan (2015)	Macedonia (2013), Nigeria (2013), Kenya (2013), Kyrgyz Republic (2013), Iraq (2014), Indonesia (2014), Kosovo (2014), Afghanistan (2015),

(continued)

[2] In the case of Slovenia, it joined the OECD in 2010 and became a member of the OECD DAC in 2013, and its first NAP was formulated in 2010, prior to its accession to the DAC.

Table 5.1 (continued)

Time periods	*OECD DAC Members adopting NAPs*	*Non-OECD DAC Members adopting NAPS*
2016–2018 Towards 20-year anniversary	Czech Republic (2017), Luxembourg (2018), Poland (2018)	Timor Leste (2016), Kenya (2016), Ukraine (2016), Palestine (2017), Niger (2017), Jordan (2017), Angola (2017), Guatemala (2017), El Salvador (2017), Cameroon (2017), Solomon Islands (2017), Brazil (2017), Montenegro (2017), Albania (2018), Tunisia (2018), Moldova (2018), Mozambique (2018)
2019–2023 SCR 1325 20-year anniversary effect	Slovakia (2020)	Yemen (2019), Bangladesh (2019), Lebanon (2019), Namibia (2019), Armenia (2019), South Africa (2020), Sudan (2020), Malta (2020), Latvia (2020), Mexico (2021), UAE (2021), South Africa (2021), Uruguay (2021), Malawi (2021), Peru (2021), Somalia (2021), Kazakhstan (2022), Morocco (2022), Chad (2023), Sri Lanka (2023)

Source Women's International League for Peace and Freedom (https://www.wilpf.org/, accessed 31 October 2023)

Germany's Outward-Looking NAPs to Implement Women, Peace and Security

In the case of Germany, the Federal Government has been publishing its NAPs to implement SCR 1325 since 2013, relatively late compared to other European countries. However, Germany is still considered one of the UN Member States that initiated its efforts to implement SCR 1325 at the national level at an early stage, as the German government published three reports to document its implementation of the resolution in 2004, 2007 and 2010, prior to the publication of its first NAP.

Currently, the fourth German NAP (2021–2024) is in force, and it emphasizes that the WPS agenda is one of the horizontal policy objectives of the German government, with the Federal Foreign Office (AA), Federal Ministry for Family Affairs, Senior Citizens, Women and Youth

(BMFSFJ), Federal Ministry of the Interior (BMI), Federal Ministry of Justice and Consumer Protection (BMJV) and Federal Ministry for Economic Cooperation and Development (BMZ) participating in its implementation (Federal Foreign Office, 2021). The involvement of BMFSFJ, BMI and BMJV, whose primary policy domain is mainly in the domestic sphere, proves the fact that the German NAP covers not only the protection of women in conflict-related settings but also domestic concerns such as the protection and reintegration of refugees and migrants in the country. Thus, in comparison to other donor countries, Germany is considered one of the best examples of a well-balanced application of both internal and external objectives in the application of WPS (Westermann, 2018).

Notwithstanding this "whole of government" approach, in practice, 31 of the 46 indicators in the six priority areas—crisis prevention, participation, protection and support; humanitarian assistance; crisis management and reconstruction; strengthening the women; peace and security agenda; and increasing institutional integration and capacities—of the fourth NAP (2021–2024) are being implemented by BMZ, indicating that the German NAP is primarily engaged externally with development cooperation efforts. In this sense, the German NAP recognizes that the German missions abroad in fragile contexts and (post-) conflict countries have a crucial responsibility to effectively drive the implementation of the WPS agenda, as do the missions in multilateral locations.

Germany's outward-looking focus of the WPS agenda is expected to be further strengthened under Olaf Scholz's current centre-left coalition government. Following the introduction of policy guidelines on its feminist foreign policy (FFP) and feminist development policy (FDP), as announced in its 2021 coalition agreement, the new FFP guidelines were launched by the Federal Foreign Office on 1 March 2023 (Federal Foreign Office, 2023). In the guidelines, the implementation and strengthening of the WPS agenda is identified as a priority for the multilateral engagement of Germany, especially as one of the key agendas in Germany's candidacy for a non-permanent seat on the Security Council for 2027–2028. With the financial commitment to allocate 85% of bilateral ODA to projects that include gender equality and women's empowerment by 2025, Germany's support for implementing the WPS in conflict-related settings is expected to increase.

South Korea's Inward Focus on Its NAPs

South Korea, in contrast to its active engagement in the promotion of the WPS agenda at the UN circle, including its participation as a founding member of the Group of Friends of Women, Peace and Security since 2001, has been rather sluggish in its attempts to embrace the WPS agenda domestically. Its first NAP was only launched in 2014 in response to a strong push from civil society through the National Assembly (Park, 2021). *Women Making Peace*, a Korean women's rights group, first launched the 1325 Peace Club in December 2006 to advocate the adoption of the NAP, but it did not achieve much success over the years (Kang, 2013). Then, in 2011, Choi Yong-hee, a chair of the Women and Family Affairs Committee at the National Assembly, passed a resolution calling for the government to draft its NAP with the support of 32 National Assembly members. In response to such demands, the Korean government led a number of consultation group meetings in preparation for drafting the NAP in 2012 (MOGEF, 2021). Shortly after the series of discussions with a small group of experts and government officials, South Korea completed drafting its first NAP and submitted it to the UN in 2014 (Yoon & Liljeström, 2022).

Following the adoption of its first NAP under the leadership of the Ministry of Foreign Affairs, the Ministry of Gender Equality and Family (MOGEF) was designated to lead the government-wide efforts to draft and implement the second (2018–2020) and third (2021–2023) NAPs. This shift in lead ministry reflects the recognition of the necessity to emphasize WPS implementation within the country. In the case of the Korea International Cooperation Agency (KOICA), a government agency dedicated to implementing South Korea's grant aid programmes, it has participated since the implementation of the second NAP in 2018 with eight ministries—Ministry of Gender Equality and Family (MOGEF), Ministry of Foreign Affairs (MOFA), Ministry of Education (MOE), Ministry of Unification (MOU), Ministry of Justice (MOJ), Ministry of National Defence (MND) and Ministry of the Interior and Safety (MOIS)—and one agency, the Korean National Police Agency (KNPA). Of the 24 action plans in the five areas being implemented—prevention, participation, protection, relief and recovery—and the monitoring of the implementation of the third NAP (2021–2023), only seven are being undertaken by KOICA.

This differs from most donor countries, including Germany, where the foreign ministry takes the lead in drafting the NAP, and ministries and agencies dealing with development cooperation are mostly responsible for implementation and monitoring. South Korea's third NAP (2021–2023) recognizes South Korea as a contributor to development assistance and mentions expanding development cooperation efforts for women and girls in conflict-related settings. The plan places considerable emphasis on the domestic context of South Korea, a country that has experienced wartime sexual violence and human rights violations from the 1930s till the end of the Second World War, as evidenced by the so-called "comfort women" who were victimized by the Japanese imperialist military (Barrow, 2016; Yoon & Liljeström, 2022). Since the Korean government considers itself as a country in conflict, where the Korean Peninsula remains divided into North and South, it has been taking a step beyond adopting the WPS agenda within its defence and foreign policy, as other donor countries such as Germany have done, and has also incorporated it in its unification policy (Yoon & Liljeström, 2022). In this regard, the National Unification Advisory Council (NUAC), the presidential consultative body in the field of unification, has been involved as one of the government agencies since the third NAP, and activities related to seeking "avenues for fostering inter-Korean cooperation on WPS and promote exchange" and taking "measures to safeguard the human rights of North Korean women defectors" are included in the document. These elements suggest that the third NAP was drafted under the Moon Jae-in administration, reflecting the progressive side's tradition of focusing on strengthening ties with North Korea. As there has been no substantive inter-Korean dialogue since the US–North Korea summit in Hanoi 2019 ended without an agreement, most of the related action plans have yet to be realized.

Future Prospects

Over the coming years, the relevance of development cooperation within Germany's implementation of the WPS agenda is expected to be further enhanced with the launch of feminist foreign policy (FFP) and feminist development policy (FDP), both of which have been framed in close consultation with civil society, parliamentarians and academics. In terms of its scope and ambition, Germany's initiative is well ahead of the group of governments that have explicitly adopted or declared a feminist perspective in their foreign and development cooperation policy since 2014, and is anticipated to take on the leading role of this group, replacing Sweden, which abandoned its groundbreaking feminist foreign policy under its new right-wing government in 2022.

Interestingly, South Korea is also likely to expand its commitment to integrating development cooperation efforts within its WPS implementation. However, this may not at all be driven by a desire related to mainstream feminist perspectives in foreign and development cooperation policy, as in Germany, but rather by somewhat coincidental political circumstances.

Given the current Yoon Suk-yeol administration's hawkish stance on North Korea, South Korea's fourth NAP, which is being formulated by the soon-to-be abolished Ministry of Gender Equality and Family, is anticipated to weaken the emphasis on WPS implementation in the peacebuilding process on the Korea Peninsula, which was highlighted in the previous NAP, drafted during the Moon administration. Instead, in light of the current administration's self-identification as a global pivotal state and its UN Security Council membership scheduled for 2024–2025, development cooperation efforts within the fourth NAP to implement the WPS agenda are expected to intensify, including increased support for victims of gender-based violence (GBV) in conflict-related settings, and financial contribution to the UN's activities related to WPS.

As a result, the expected paradox is that the Yoon administration, which is retrogressing decades of progress in gender equality policies in South Korea, is positioning itself as a proponent of the WPS agenda in the international community, and such contradiction is a reflection of the international community's expectations of South Korea's foreign policy over the long run.

References

Barrow, A. (2016). Operationalizing Security Council Resolution 1325: The role of national action plans. *Journal of Conflict and Security Law, 21*(2), 247–275. https://doi.org/10.1093/jcsl/krw002

Birkenkötter, H. (2021). *Taking stock: A review of Germany's two years on the Security Council*. Völkerrechtsblog. https://nbn-resolving.org/urn:nbn:de:0301-20210125-191100-0-9

Federal Foreign Office. (2021). *The German Federal Government's action plan for the women, peace and security agenda 2021 to 2024*. https://www.auswaertiges-amt.de/blob/610626/d7d78947490f454a5342c1dff737a474/aktionsplan1325-engl-data.pdf

Federal Foreign Office. (2023). *Shaping feminist foreign policy: Federal foreign office guidelines*. https://www.auswaertiges-amt.de/blob/2585008/d444590d5a7741acc6e37a142959170e/ll-ffp-data.pdf

Fröhlich, M. (2023). *50 years of Germany in the United Nations: Initiatives, continuities and change in German UN Policy*. Federal Foreign Office. https://www.auswaertiges-amt.de/en/sr-mitgliedschaft/391348

George, N., & Shepherd, L. J. (2016). Women, peace and security: Exploring the implementation and integration of UNSCR 1325. *International Political Science Review, 37*(3), 297–306.

Jung, Y., & Tsujisaka, A. (2019). *Emerging actors in the women, peace and security agenda: South Korea and Japan*. Stockholm International Peace Research Institute. https://www.sipri.org/publications/2019/sipri-background-papers/emerging-actors-women-peace-and-security-agenda-south-korea-and-japan

Kang, Y. (2013). The formulation and implementation of international norms on women, peace and security: UN Security Council Resolution 1325. *Journal of World Politics, 19*, 55–96. https://s-space.snu.ac.kr/handle/10371/94965

Ministry of Gender Equality and Family. (2021). *The Third National Action Plan of the Republic of Korea for the implementation of United Nations Security Council Resolution 1325 on women, peace, and security*. https://www.mogef.go.kr/sp/geq/sp_geq_f014.do. Accessed 28 October 2023.

Muehlenhoff, H. L. (2022). Unpacking the making of National Action Plans: Governmentality, security, and race in the Dutch implementation of UNSCR 1325. *International Feminist Journal of Politics, 24*(5), 744–766. https://doi.org/10.1080/14616742.2022.2042353

OECD (Organisation for Economic Cooperation and Development). (2020). *Twentieth anniversary of UN Security Council Resolution 1325: Financing gender equality and women's empowerment in fragile contexts*. www.oecd.org/development/gender-development/OECD-Gendernet-Financing-UNSCR.pdf

OECD Creditor Reporting System (CRS). (2023). https://stats.oecd.org/Index.aspx?DataSetCode=crs1. Accessed 25 October 2023.

Park, M. J. (2021). Women, peace, and security norm diffusion in international development cooperation policy: A comparative analysis of the UK and South Korea. *International Development and Cooperation Review, 13*(2), 121–135. https://doi.org/10.32580/idcr.2021.13.2.121

Popovic, N. (2020). *The other side of the mirror: Perceptions of Germany's commitment to women, peace and security*. Gender Associations. https://www.auswaertiges-amt.de/blob/2408770/25fc046fd9df6f9e2075a39fad969df4/201022-studie-wps-data.pdf. Accessed 30 October 2023.

Shepherd, L. J. (2016). Making war safe for women? National action plans and the militarisation of the women, peace and security agenda. *International Political Science Review, 37*(3), 324–335.

Swaine, A. (2009). Assessing the potential of national action plans to advance implementation of United Nations Security Council Resolution 1325. *Yearbook of International Humanitarian Law, 12*, 403–433. https://doi.org/10.1017/S1389135909000142. Accessed 26 October 2023.

Tryggestad, T. L. (2009). Trick or treat? The UN and implementation of Security Council Resolution 1325 on women, peace, and security. *Global Governance, 15*(4), 539–557.

Westermann, J. (2018). WPS 2018: Common challenges for NAP development—Germany and Australia. *The Strategist*. https://www.aspistrategist.org.au/wps-2018-common-challenges-nap-development-germany-australia/. Accessed 2 November 2023.

Yoon, J., & Liljeström, L. (2022). 1325 NAPs beyond East and West: Institutionalizing the WPS agenda in Sweden and South Korea. *Focus Asia: Perspective & Analysis*. https://isdp.eu/content/uploads/2022/03/1325-NAPs-Beyond-East-and-West-Institutionalizing-the-WPS-Agenda-in-Sweden-and-South-Korea-1.pdf. Accessed 3 November 2023.

PART II

Regional and Global Contexts

CHAPTER 6

The Impact of Geopolitics on the Field of Development in Korea and Germany

Brendan Howe and Stephan Klingebiel

Abstract Geopolitical tensions are omnipresent in all areas of international relations, in theory and in practice. This also applies to the field of development discourse, including in the discussions in September 2023 on the (lack of) progress made towards realizing the 2030 Agenda and in the specific development policies and initiatives of individual governments. This chapter analyses how the dynamic international context is influencing the development policy approaches of OECD countries and of two donor countries in particular: the Republic of Korea (hereafter

The authors are grateful to Niels Keijzer's feedback on an earlier draft of the chapter.

B. Howe
Ewha Womans University, Seoul, Korea
e-mail: howeb@ewha.ac.kr

S. Klingebiel (✉)
German Institute of Development and Sustainability (IDOS), Bonn, Germany
e-mail: Stephan.Klingebiel@idos-research.de

S. Klingebiel et al. (eds.), *Emerging Trends in International Development and Climate Policy*,
https://doi.org/10.1007/978-3-031-65671-2_6

referred to as Korea) and Germany. It analyses the overall geopolitical context and strategies of both countries, and the intersection of geopolitics and geoeconomics. Geographically, the piece pays special attention to the Indo-Pacific Region. It discusses how far development policy in Germany is dependent upon or independent of the geostrategic approaches of the two donor countries.

Keywords Geopolitical tensions · Geopolitics · Geoeconomics · International relations · Development policy · Donor countries · Indo-Pacific Region · Republic of Korea · Germany · China · OECD · Global South · BRICS

Introduction

Geopolitics has always been a factor in development debates and development cooperation, and we should not expect this to change (Liao & Lee, 2022; Nath & Klingebiel, 2023; Power, 2019). During the Cold War, ideologically competing powers used development cooperation as a political soft-power tool to fight or cultivate communism. Korea, for example, received generous support from the US due to its geostrategic location in Asia and south of the Soviet-backed Democratic People's Republic of Korea (North Korea). Similarly, the Soviet Union (USSR) supported China and Mongolia with large-scale infrastructure projects and signed the "Treaty of Peace, Friendship and Co-operation" with India in 1971. In the 1960s, poverty became a global problem and richer countries began to address the basic needs of poorer countries. In 1961, the Development Assistance Committee of the Organisation for Economic Co-operation and Development (OECD DAC) was established as the main donor forum for coordinating aid from developed countries to developing countries (Bracho et al., 2021). Containing the influence of the Eastern Bloc was a major driving force behind the creation of the DAC (Nath & Klingebiel, 2023).

Far-reaching geopolitical upheavals have characterized international relations in the recent past. The systemic confrontation between China and the US, the Russian invasion of Ukraine, the seizure of power during military coups in Niger, as well as earlier in Mali and Burkina Faso, and the complete takeover of Afghanistan by the Taliban reveal that the environment for global cooperation efforts has become much more difficult. Global cooperation has taken considerable steps backwards in recent months or years. Populism and autocratic trends in all regions of the world are seriously damaging global cooperation efforts. Scope for finding common solutions—above all in combating climate change—is difficult or even impossible, and in turn itself forms part of international lines of conflict (Klingebiel, 2023). Indeed, there are concerns that geopolitical concerns and fractures pose a fatal impediment to multilateralism (Howe, 2023).

The Global South is to a considerable extent the scene of these conflicts of a political, economic, and often also military nature. In an essential departure from earlier periods, however, countries of the Global South (Haug et al., 2021)—while not a homogeneous group—are now essential co-shapers in international relations (Ishmael (Ed.), 2022). This applies first and foremost to China, but also to India and other actors from the BRICS group and beyond. Beyond large non-OECD G20 members such as India, South Africa and Brazil, the behaviour of smaller states towards Russia and China is of considerable international importance, as shown by the votes in the United Nations General Assembly, or participation in Chinese development initiatives. This is why development paradigms and development policy approaches by Western countries as well as South–South Cooperation providers play a crucial role in this changing context.

The geopolitical upheavals of recent years ultimately affect all policies of OECD countries. Germany and Korea are both members of the OECD, which is typically regarded as the crucial economic coordination platforms of "Western countries" (Bracho et al., 2021). The geographical, political and economic context of both countries is in many ways different, with Korea being part of the Indo-Pacific and Northeast Asia subregion, whereas Germany is very much rooted in the European Union. Both countries have important commonalities, too, such as their strong economic export orientation and close economic links with China.

The new geopolitical trends apply to the classic fields of foreign and security policy, climate and energy policy, but also increasingly to other policy fields, such as the agricultural and science policies of OECD countries. A fundamental aspect of Western development policy is its focus on the Global South. This is a fundamental characteristic and rationale of the policy field (Klingebiel, 2022a). In this respect, the question is of great importance: What does all this mean for development policy concepts and narratives, and likewise for operational implementation?

The Indo-Pacific Region in the Approaches of Germany and Korea

The Indo-Pacific region,[1] which stretches from the Indian Ocean to the Pacific Ocean and includes India, is gaining importance in academic and policy debates. Most countries of the region belong to the "Global South", and some countries to the OECD (Australia, Japan and Korea). Korea, a country which belonged only 25 years ago to the Global South and was heavily dependent on Official Development Assistance (ODA) for 50 years (1945–1995), plays a special role because of its recent graduation (Howe, 2017: 249).

The Indo-Pacific region accounts for approximately 40% of global GDP, is expected to be the biggest contributor to global growth for the next decades, and sharpens all dimensions of global affairs (security, trade, etc.). Top global economies are based in the Indo-Pacific: China (global economic rank #2), Japan (#4), India (#5), Korea (#13), Australia (#14) and Indonesia (#16). The region is home to 60% of the world's population.

China's expanding geopolitical, economic and investment footprint has resulted in multiple strategies, designed implicitly or explicitly to counter China's rising influence. These include multipronged Indo-Pacific strategies and approaches from Australia, Canada, France, Germany, Japan, Korea, India, the Netherlands, UK, the EU, the US and ASEAN (Association of Southeast Asian Nations). There is no relevant OECD actor without a current Indo-Pacific strategy, including the US (White House, 2022), the European Union (Joint Communication by European Commission and the High Representative of the Union for Foreign Affairs and Security Policy, 2021), Korea (December 2022), and the German government guidelines on the Indo-Pacific region (2020). The latest US National Security Strategy (October 2022) mentions the region 32 times. Increasing attention for the region indicates a higher level of

[1] World regions are imagined and constructed. They are based on perceptions, positions, interests and changing contexts. Regions can be determined by geographical features and based on geopolitical and geoeconomic interests of actors. This is also true for a recent term that is increasingly used: the "Indo-Pacific" or the "Indo-Pacific region". While the term "Indo-Pacific" was introduced by Japanese Prime Minister Shinzo Abe in 2007 (who introduced the concept in a speech in New Delhi, India), it has been increasingly used by US governments and regional actors such as ASEAN over the past decade. The term "Indo-Pacific" often replaces the term "Asia–Pacific" (Nath & Klingebiel, 2023).

geopolitical and economic competition between actors and more sensitive issues for countries expected to benefit from development policies. Many of the responses to China's challenge have focused primarily on "minilateral" hard security cooperation between three to five like-minded states led by the US (Howe, 2023).

For OECD actors there are three main motivations to focus on the region (DGAP, 2024; Klingebiel, 2022b):

1. **Economic dimension in terms of trade and supply chains**: For example, the EU and China are close trading partners. In 2021 China alone was the third most important partner of EU exports (10.2%) and the largest partner for imports (22.4%).
2. **Security dimension**: Taiwan's security; China's militarization of the South China Sea; conflicts beyond the direct involvement of China and the neighbouring countries, such as the long-lasting tense situation between India and Pakistan.
3. **Climate change dimension**: Dynamic economies of the region are among the main global carbon emitters. China alone is responsible for around 30% of all global emissions, India's global share is around 6% and Indonesia's 5%.

The Indo-Pacific focus is linked in large parts to China. However, it goes well beyond China. Major OECD actors follow a strategy, which frames China and related sectoral areas in three different ways:

1. **China as a partner**: The country is needed to meet all regional and global challenges. There is no way to work effectively on the issue of climate change or protection without China's involvement.
2. **China as a competitor**: In many cases, the country competes with OECD actors. Competitive patterns are relevant, for example, when it comes to access to raw materials (e.g. in Africa), markets (e.g. in Asia), or political influence (e.g. Asia, Pacific). Competitive features can be observed in many parts of the African continent, among others.
3. **China as a rival or a threat**: The country is increasingly perceived as offensive and/or aggressive in some areas. This includes, for instance, the militarization of the South China Sea and the relationship with Taiwan. The term "sharp power" (Nye, 2018) is used to

describe China's (and Russia's) attempts to manipulate and manage information in other countries. "Geoeconomics" as a concept is a strategy of offering economic benefits (e.g. in the context of BRI) to target other countries to influence them.

Development policy has consequently become framed within these geopolynomic narratives. "Geopolynomic" is a term introduced to encompass the intersectorality of geopolitics, geoeconomics, geostrategy, geohistory and other approaches (Howe, 2022). This becomes apparent when analysing the strategies of Germany and Korea towards the region.

Germany

In September 2020, the German government launched its strategy (actually called "guidelines") on the Indo-Pacific region. To set itself apart from former German approaches, the document emphasizes strongly German "interests" in the region. The document actually starts with (i) interests (such as "peace and security" and "open markets and free trade") and discusses in addition (ii) principles (such as "multilateralism" and "European action") and (iii) initiatives (for example, for tackling climate change). The strategy reflects on sustainable development concepts (SDGs, etc.) and to a certain extent on Germany's development policy approach in the region without giving this policy field much explicit attention. Based on the document from 2020, the German government publishes, on an annual basis, progress reports on the implementation of its Indo-Pacific region strategy.

The release of the first China strategy in mid-July 2023 sparked significant debate in Germany, particularly when compared to the Indo-Pacific region strategy. Conflicts arose in the preparation of the document and the follow-up discussions between those actors in Germany favouring concrete interests (maintaining good trade relationship, etc.) and those highlighting "values" (such as the human rights situation in China). Some of these conflicts were between actors within the German federal government, and also linked to the development of a national security strategy which was prepared in parallel to the China strategy. However, many debates also showed that reality is in many ways much more complex. For instance, an economic de-risking strategy goes beyond a binary distinction between interests and values.

The presence and history of Indo-Pacific engagement of France and the UK is more intense than that of Germany; at the same time there are several similarities (Paskal, 2021). One similarity is the concern that national policies are fractured into two groupings. For a long period, some sections of political and economic communities were looking for closer ties with China, while defence, intelligence and security communities were concerned about China's influence and strategies domestically and internationally.

Against a background that the Indo-Pacific region strategies of Germany and other OECD countries are at least implicitly driven by China's rise over recent years, this document is more explicit on Germany's view and policy approach. The document uses a three-category approach (very similar to the overall OECD framing) for dealing with China: China as a partner, as a competitor and as a systemic rival. The document does not spell out in which category it puts the field of "development" (including China's development initiatives) and "development policy" (see also Nath & Klingebiel, 2023).

Interestingly, development topics play a crucial role in the German China strategy. Given the fact that China's rise is closely related to its development paradigm and its connectivity and infrastructure approach (not least to the Belt and Road Initiative, launched in 2013) the strategy reflects on the topic in several ways. This includes the geoeconomic potential of China's development initiatives (using trade, finance, etc., for geopolitical purposes). The strategy also presents some areas of continued cooperation in the field of development policy between Germany and China (such as specific triangular cooperation activities and academic collaboration related to development topics).

In addition to the overall strategies of the Federal Government, the German Federal Ministry of Economic Cooperation and Development (BMZ) launched a new strategy on "German development policy with Asia" in December 2023. Interestingly, the paper does not use the Indo-Pacific region as a framing regional concept. And the document emphasizes mainly the topics for Germany's general development policy since the governing coalition came into power in December 2021. Thus, the guiding aspects of the BMZ Asia strategy are "innovation", "social" and "feminist".

Finally, yet importantly, Germany pushes to a large extent connectivity and infrastructure initiatives of the EU, the G7 and beyond. Those initiatives are implicitly, and often even explicitly, responding to China's engagement in this regard. They typically emphasize the aspects of high-quality infrastructure and sustainability, and sometimes refer to a different set of values coming along the investments.

Those activities include the Global Gateway initiative of the European Union (see the chapter by Keijzer in this volume) and the G7 Partnership for Global Infrastructure and Investment, launched under Germany's G7 presidency in 2022, and brings together several initiatives of the EU, Japan and the US. The Western connectivity and infrastructure initiatives, such as the Global Gateway, include public development funding, but they go beyond public resources and intend to mobilize private sector investments.

Korea

Much of the internal perception of South Korea, as well as the external strategic analysis of its policy options, has focused on the relative weakness and vulnerability of the country in what has been described as one of the most dangerous regions in the world (Calder & Ye, 2010). Indeed, it had long seemed the geostrategic destiny of the country to suffer the fate of a shrimp in the old Korean proverb and get crushed to death in the fight between whales, as has been repeatedly referenced by commentators from all political and paradigmatic backgrounds, across an extended analytical period (Kim, 2006; Lee & Park, 2017; Shim, 2009).

In terms of strategic discourse, the shrimp among whales narrative finds the greatest support from a power political or "realist" view of the world, wherein a small weak state, surrounded by regional and global behemoths, has severely limited options, in the face of a geostrategic operating environment within which, to quote Thucydides (c. 413 BCE), the "the strong do what they can and the weak suffer what they must". Available strategies are traditionally restricted to "balancing' or "bandwagoning" with the strong. Yet, such are the geostrategic and geoeconomics constraints upon Korea, that the country has been conceptualized as being stuck between a "rock and a hard place' in terms of its military dependency upon its closest ally, the US, and its largest market and trading partner, China (Kim & Cha, 2016). Pressured by the US strategic "rebalancing" in the region, and China's geostrategic "wedge" policy platform, rather than balancing or bandwagoning with either, often Korea, has tried to operationalize some form of "hedging" strategy (Chun & Ku, 2010; Kang, 2009; Kim, 2021).

Ultimately this approach was also abandoned with the inauguration of the Yoon Suk-yeol administration. Prior to coming to power President Yoon had made it clear that "rebuilding" Korea's alliance with the US was to be central to his geostrategic policy commitments and was also a recognition of Washington's frustrations with the hedging of the outgoing government of President Moon Jae-in (Lee, 2022). Yoon has come off the fence and chosen sides between the whales. For Ramon Pardo, the extent to which this was ever in doubt has been exaggerated by other commentators; he posts that, rather than a strategic dilemma, Seoul was faced with a strategic non-dilemma, and had "long ago decided that when it comes to foreign policy and security, its past, present, and future lies with the US and other like-minded partners" (Pardo, 2022). To try to create some policy space within these hierarchical power constraints, successive Korean governments have striven for a geopolynomic niche role.

The Roh Moo-hyun administration (2003–2008) projected South Korea's pivotal role as a "balancer" or "hub" in the region to facilitate regional cooperation in the realms of economy and security (Cheong, 2008). During the Lee Myung-bak administration (2008–2013), South Korea's self-identification as a middle power took a more explicit form (Teo, 2018). Under the overarching slogan of "Global Korea", the concept of middle power was used to support the aspiration to increase the country's international influence by enhancing its networking capacity and convening power (Green, 2017). The Park Guen-hye administration (2014–2016) was more reluctant to apply the middle-power nomenclature to its diplomatic posture due to fear of provoking apprehension and/or misunderstanding in the US and China. Yet, even though the use of middle-power language started to diminish early in Park's term, related geostrategic policies were still pursued, such as the establishment of the middle-power grouping of Mexico, Indonesia, Korea, Turkey and Australia (MIKTA), and the promotion of the Northeast Asia Peace and Cooperation Initiative (Lee & Park, 2017). Among the public and academics in Korea and abroad, the terminology has also been used to describe Korea's "middle" position between China and the US under progressive administrations in Seoul, peaking with Moon Jae-in's hedging and bridging endeavours (Kim & Cha, 2016).

Despite abandoning the "betwixt" conceptualizations of Korea's geostrategic position of his predecessors, Yoon Suk-yeol's "Global Pivotal State" owes much to their ideational legacy. The details of the policy platform imply a continuation of the broadening of middle-power aspirations and niche diplomatic activities begun by previous administrations to include non-strategic initiatives. But they also reflect an enhanced aspirational role for a Korea seen as more influential than a "mere" middle power. The combination of hard power and soft power in the contemporary discourse is termed "smart power", and these areas of foreign policy platform construction have been of particular importance in the middle-power discourse (Center for Strategic & International Studies, 2007). Given their lack of compulsory power, middle powers need to pursue "niche diplomacy", which involves concentrating resources in specific areas best able to generate returns worth having, rather than trying to cover the field, allowing them, therefore, to "punch above their weight" (Henrikson, 2005: 67).

The proposal of the administration of Moon Jae-in (2017–2022) for a Northeast Asia Peace Community (NEAPC) contained three components: a Northeast Asia Peace and Cooperation Platform (NAPCP), a New Northern Policy (NNP) and a New Southern Policy (NSP). The ambitious aim was to build a sustainable regional system of cooperation with the 10 Member States of the Association of Southeast Asian Nations (ASEAN), the middle-power grouping of MIKTA, India and Northeast Asian states. President Yoon Yoon rebranded the Moon administration's New Southern Policy as the Korea–ASEAN Solidarity Initiative (KASI), and has consistently emphasized ASEAN's significance as an economic and strategic partner. Engagement with the "South" was initially termed an "ABCD Strategy" of advancing human capital, building health security, connecting cultures and digitizing Asian infrastructure, continuing the previous administration's focus on people, peace and prosperity. Hence, Yoon's "Indo-Pacific strategy upholds the notion of ASEAN centrality, and promotes ASEAN and its various mechanisms at the central platform for regional cooperation" (Ryu, 2023, p. 11).

The RoK has a significant history of liberal middle-power advocacy in terms of promoting peace, the environment and development in the Global South. Within the Indo-Pacific, Korea has consistently concentrated 30% of its total Official Development Assistance (ODA) on countries within ASEAN. Korea has 26 priority development partners, of which the largest geographical concentration is in Asia (11 countries), with six in Southeast Asia. For Soyeun Kim (2011, p. 805), "the Korean ODA model in particular epitomises Seoul's strategic positioning (or bridging) between the developed and developing countries. With the model, Korea promotes its distinctive approach to aid while at the same time proclaiming its willingness to be part of global aid efforts". Even before joining the OECD DAC, "Korea had emerged as the unrivalled leading donor, in absolute amounts, among non-DAC OECD countries" (Chun et al., 2010, p. 790).

In recent years Korea has turned its attention to humanitarian or principled diplomatic and development engagement with Cambodia, Laos, Myanmar and Vietnam (the CLMV countries). Each of these countries is affected by conflict, and given the high prevalence of poverty has great need for Korean assistance. Korea has made Cambodia, Laos and Vietnam priority partners, and already has extensive humanitarian commitments in Cambodia and Vietnam. Korea has, as yet, only a limited partnership with Myanmar and Laos. The 2019 Commemorative Summit in Busan, however, also served as the First Mekong–Republic of Korea Summit. According to the official publication on the summit, recognizing the growth potential of the region, Korea has cooperated with Mekong countries in a host of areas related to humanitarian niche diplomacy such as public health, rural development and infrastructure.

Since 2017, Korea's ODA/GNI ratio has been relatively stable. Korea committed to reaching an ODA/GNI ratio of 0.2% by 2020, but the government acknowledged its failure to reach the target in the Midterm Strategy for Development Cooperation (2021–2025), citing worsening public finances. Even this target was rather low when compared to other major OECD economies (Keijzer et. al., 2022: 3). Yet President Yoon aspires to Korea playing a "leading role in the areas that necessitate our part", and "when we are asked by the international community to participate more, we need to firmly demonstrate our attitude of respect for the international rules-based order".

Korea has been criticized for focusing too greatly on bilateral rather than multilateral assistance, with the notable exception of the Green Climate Fund, which is based in the country. Given that from one perspective middle-power activism is all about visibility on the international stage, it is not surprising that Korea clings to bilateralism rather than multilateralism. Yet, President Yoon has repeatedly emphasized a desire to work with like-minded partners, so even if multilateralism is not appealing, minilateral geopolynomic cooperation might be an option for the future.

Conclusion

One crucial turning point has been and is the use of the development initiatives initiated by China for offensive geopolitics in the Global South, especially since the 2017 Communist Party Congress (Klingebiel, 2023; Nath & Klingebiel, 2023). The Belt and Road Initiative (BRI), which has been implemented since 2013, has set new standards and expectations for how an infrastructure initiative can massively change countries. Incidentally, this initiative is not only aimed at developing countries, but encompasses a total of 180 countries and institutions. The BRI is a major contributor to raising the profile of the Indo-Pacific region for actors outside and inside the region. However, the role of the region in terms of economic status and future economic potential, population size and the geopolitical power of political actors, is highly related to China, but also goes far beyond the role of the country.

Other Chinese initiatives have been added in recent years, including the Global Development Initiative (GDI) (2021), which is valued by many developing countries. At the beginning of 2023, the Global Security Initiative (GSI), agreed on by the group of BRICS countries (Brazil, Russia, India, China and South Africa), was added. The Global Civilization Initiative (GCI), published in March 2023, shows the range of the initiatives and the close links between them.

OECD actors' Indo-Pacific policies show evolution from an initially supportive view of China's South–South cooperation, to considering it a key element of the struggle for power in international relations. This is particularly true of the BRI. The Russian invasion of February 2022 acted as an extreme accelerator of overarching trends. This applies above all to the dimensions of geopolitics, geoeconomics and especially to energy and raw material security.

Germany and Korea are both aiming to reinvent their respective identities in international relations. Germany is trying to find its own role as a country with some expectations to shape international agendas. To some extent, in a similar way, Korea is developing further its role as a pivotal state.

Both countries are changing their development approaches in this new context. They have distinct regional and sub-regional geopolynomic rationales as actors within the EU/Europe and NATO on the one hand, and being a divided country in the Indo-Pacific region, based in Northeast Asia, with close economic ties to China and Japan on the other hand. Yet, to a certain degree, the OECD and its role for development topics and development policy coordination links both countries. The US likewise strongly impacts German and Korean politics, not least through the crucial role it fulfils of providing military protection to both countries.

References

Bracho, G., Carey, R., Hynes, W., Klingebiel, S., & Trzeciak-Duval, A. (Eds.). (2021). *Origins, evolution and future of global development cooperation: The role of the Development Assistance Committee (DAC)* (Studies 104). German Development Institute/Deutsches Institut für Entwicklungspolitik (DIE).

Calder, K., & Ye, M. (2010). *The making of Northeast Asia*. Stanford University Press.

Center for Strategic and International Studies. (2007). *CSIS Commission on smart power: A smarter, more secure America*. Center for Strategic and International Studies. https://carnegieendowment.org/files/csissmartpowerreport.pdf

Cheong, I. (2008). The progress of Korea's FTA policy in the context of Northeast Asian Economic Cooperation. In J. Park, T. J. Pempel, & G. Roland (Eds.), *Political economy of Northeast Asian regionalism: Political conflict and economic integration* (pp. 56–66). Edward Elgar.

Chun, J., & Ku, Y. (2010). Clashing geostrategic choices in East Asia, 2009–2015: Re-balancing, wedge strategy, and hedging. *Korean Journal of International Studies, 18*(1), 33–57.

Chun, H., Munyi, E., & Lee, H. (2010). South Korea as an emerging donor: Challenges and changes on its entering OECD/DAC. *Journal of International Development, 22*(6), 788–802.

DGAP. (2024). *Managing risks in the EU-China economic relationship*. https://dgap.org/en/research/publications/managing-risks-eu-china-economic-relationship. Accessed 16 January 2024.

European Commission. (2021). *Joint communication to the European parliament and the council: The EU strategy for the cooperation in the Indo-Pacific*. https://www.eeas.europa.eu/eeas/joint-communication-indo-pacific_en

Green, M. (2017). Korean middle power diplomacy and Asia's emerging multilateral architecture. In V. Cha & M. DuMond (Eds.), *The Korean pivot: The study of South Korea as a global power* (pp. 17–34). Center for Strategic and International Studies.

Haug, S., Braveboy-Wagner, J., & Maihold, G. (2021). The "Global South" in the study of world politics: Examining a meta category. *Third World Quarterly, 42*(9), 1923–1944. https://doi.org/10.1080/01436597.2020.1712999

Henrikson, A. (2005). Niche diplomacy in the world public arena: The global "corners" of Canada and Norway. In J. Melissen (Ed.), *The new public diplomacy: Soft power in international relations* (pp. 67–87). Palgrave Macmillan.

Howe, B. (2017). Korea's role for peace-building and development in Asia. *Asian Journal of Peacebuilding, 5*(2), 243–266.

Howe, B. (2022). Future direction of Korean geopolynomic positioning. *Jeju Forum Journal, 3*, 23–34.

Howe, B. (2023). East Asian security cooperation shortcomings and opportunities for second-tier actors in the region. *Journal of East Asian Affairs, 36*(1), 39–78.

Ishmael, L. (Ed.). (2022). *Aftermath of war in Europe: The West vs. the Global South?* Policy Center for the New South.

Kang, D. (2009). Between balancing and bandwagoning: South Korea's response to China. *Journal of East Asian Studies, 9*(1), 1–28.

Keijzer, N., Klingebiel, S., & Oh, M. J. (2022). *Learning from each other: The multifaceted potential for partnership between the Republic of Korea and Germany* (IDOS Policy Brief 13/2022). German Institute of Development and Sustainability. https://www.idos-research.de/uploads/media/PB_13.2022.pdf

Kim, M. (2021). Hedging between the United States and China? South Korea's ideology-driven behavior and its implications for national security. *International Relations of the Asia-Pacific*. https://doi.org/10.1093/irap/lcab020

Kim, S. (2006). *The two Koreas and the great powers*. Cambridge University Press.

Kim, S. (2011). Bridging troubled worlds? An analysis of the ethical case for South Korean aid. *Journal of International Development, 23*, 802–822.

Kim, E., & Cha, V. (2016). Between a rock and a hard place: South Korea's strategic dilemmas with China and the United States. *Asia Policy, 21*, 101–121. http://www.nbr.org/publications/asia_policy/free/120516/AsiaPolicy21_Kim_Cha_January2016.pdf

Klingebiel, S. (2022a). *Engaging with partners in the Global South in uncertain times* (Policy Brief 5/2022). German Institute of Development and Sustainability (IDOS). https://doi.org/10.23661/ipb5.2022

Klingebiel, S. (2022b). Development cooperation and climate change: The quest for orientation in a challenging context. *Development Cooperation Review, 5*(1), 3–12.

Klingebiel, S. (2023). *Geopolitics, the Global South and development policy* (IDOS Policy Brief 14/2023).

Lee, M. (2022). South Korean President-elect Yoon Suk-yeol unveils foreign policy goals. *Washington Post*. https://www.washingtonpost.com/world/2022/04/14/south-korea-president-interview/

Lee, S., & Park, C. (2017). Korea's middle power diplomacy for human security: A global and regional approach. *Journal of International and Area Studies, 24*(1), 21–44.

Liao, C., & Lee, B. (2022). *The geopolitics of development in building global prosperity: Proposals for sustainable growth*. Chatham House. https://www.chathamhouse.org/2022/12/building-global-prosperity/03-geopolitics-development

Nath, E., & Klingebiel, S. (2023). *Geopolitical competition in the Indo-Pacific: Managing development cooperation* (Policy Brief 8/2023). German Institute of Development and Sustainability (IDOS). https://doi.org/10.23661/ipb8.2023

Nye, J. (2018). How sharp power threatens soft power, the right and wrong ways to respond to authoritarian influence. *Foreign Affairs*. https://www.foreignaffairs.com/articles/china/2018-01-24/how-sharp-power-threatens-soft-power

Paskal, C. (2021). *Indo-Pacific strategies, perceptions and partnership: The view from seven countries*. Chatham House. https://www.chathamhouse.org/2021/03/indo-pacific-strategies-perceptions-and-partnerships/01-introduction

Pardo, R. (2022). *South Korea as a "global pivotal state": The role of partners* (CSDS Policy Brief). https://brussels-school.be/sites/default/files/CSDS%20Policy%20brief_2207_0.pdf

Power, M. (2019). *Geopolitics and development*. Routledge.

Ryu, Y. (2023). South Korea in 2022: Aspiring to become a global pivotal state. *East Asian Policy, 15*(1), 7–21.

Shim, D. (2009). A shrimp amongst whales? Assessing South Korea's regional power status. In *Power, norms and governance in international relations*. GIGA Research Programme.

Teo, S. (2018). Middle power identities of Australia and South Korea: Comparing the Kevin Rudd/Julia Gillard and Lee Myung-bak administration. *The Pacific Review, 31*(2), 221–239.

White House. (2022). *Indo-Pacific strategy of the United States*. Washington, D.C. https://www.whitehouse.gov/wp-content/uploads/2022/02/U.S.-Indo-Pacific-Strategy.pdf

CHAPTER 7

The Southernization of the EU's Development Policy? A Critical Review of the EU Global Gateway

Niels Keijzer

Abstract In December 2019, the newly elected European Commission (EU) President tasked one of her Commissioners to ensure that the EU's approach to development cooperation would evolve in line with new global realities, while contributing to the EU's wider political priorities. Two summers and a pandemic later, the Commission announced its Global Gateway initiative. This proposal sought to strengthen the EU's visibility and impact in the area of infrastructure investment, and committed the EU and its member states to jointly mobilize EUR 300 billion in investment during the period 2022 to 2030. This chapter discusses the emergence of this initiative in relation to the literature on

The author would like to thank Stephan Klingebiel and Emma Mawdsley for their feedback on an earlier version of this chapter.

N. Keijzer (✉)
German Institute of Development and Sustainability (IDOS), Bonn, Germany
e-mail: niels.keijzer@idos-research.de

S. Klingebiel et al. (eds.), *Emerging Trends in International Development and Climate Policy*,
https://doi.org/10.1007/978-3-031-65671-2_7

the "southernization" of the OECD members' development policies. It observes that Global Gateway has since become the defining feature in the EU's international partnerships policy and has become ubiquitous in its public discourse. Its effects on public expectations of development policy may thus be greater than the changes in approaches "on the ground". The chapter concludes by discussing the policy relevance of Global Gateway for the development policy and operations of Korea and Germany.

Keywords European Commission · EU · Global Gateway initiative · Infrastructure · Development policy · International partnerships · Republic of Korea · Germany

Introduction

At the turn of the millennium, development policy appeared to witness its "end of history" moment, to borrow Fukuyama's (in)famous phrase. The United Nations' Millennium Declaration and its eight Millennium Development Goals were strongly influenced by a document issued by the Development Assistance Committee (DAC) of the OECD a few years before (OECD/DAC, 1996). The 9/11 terror attacks only added to the Western world's resolve to strengthen international development cooperation, at that time characterized by growing budgets and a stronger appetite for reform and collective action. The members of the OECD and like-minded international organizations made efforts to promote a "social contract" for development through subsequent high-level fora on aid effectiveness. From 2005 to 2011, dedicated efforts were made to involve emerging countries and their expanding international cooperation efforts, which in all their diversity are referred to as South–South Cooperation (SSC).

Two decades further on, the situation looks markedly different and the international competition for influence—referred to as "the politics of generosity" by the EU's High-Representative for foreign and security policy (Borrell, 2020)—continues to increase. Since the start of the pandemic in 2020, the development policies of OECD members increasingly emphasize "mutual benefits" in their policy statements (Keijzer & Lundsgaarde, 2018) and more explicitly focus on promoting own interests in addition to developing country benefits. These policy shifts have been described as the "southernization" of development policy (Mawdsley, 2018).[1]

Among the clearest indications of this southernization was the launch of the European Union's Global Gateway, a policy initiative announced by the European Commission President in September 2021 in her annual policy speech to the European Parliament. During this policy speech, she positioned the initiative as a direct response to China's Belt and Road Initiative (BRI) as follows:

> We are good at financing roads. But it does not make sense for Europe to build a perfect road between a Chinese-owned copper mine and a Chinese-owned harbour. We have to get smarter when it comes to these kinds of investments.
>
> This is why we will soon present our new connectivity strategy called Global Gateway. (Von der Leyen, 2021, p. 15)

This chapter describes the genesis and implementation of Global Gateway to date, and critically reviews the initiative in relation to similar policy debates in Germany and Korea. It first looks into the literature on the "southernization" of the OECD members' development policies. It subsequently discusses Global Gateway and the EU policy discussions from where it sprang, in reference to similar policy discussions in German and Korea.

The Southernization of Development Policy

Germany was one of the founding members of the DAC in 1961. Korea joined the Committee in 2010, almost half a century later and in a very different time and age. At that time, one year had passed since the Lehman Brothers Bank filed for bankruptcy and signalled the start of the global economic and financial crisis. In the period leading up to this crisis, efforts were made by the OECD to increase cooperation with the group of "emerging donors", principally China and India as leading SSC providers, seeking to promote convergence between their policies and practice and those promoted by the DAC members (Mawdsley, 2018). The trio of High-Level Fora on Aid Effectiveness, held in

[1] A new publication has since proposed the "Easternization" of development policy as an alternative term to refer to the same phenomenon (Ito, 2023).

Accra (2008), Busan (2011) and Paris (2005), served as key moments to promote this convergence, particularly with discussions in the run-up to Busan seeking to "enlarge the tent" of those subscribing to the development effectiveness agenda's principles and objectives. The efforts were however largely unsuccessful, with the Busan outcome document including a non-committal reference to SSC providers applying the agreed principles on a voluntary basis (Eyben & Savage, 2013).

Instead of the desired convergence of SSC policies and practices to those of the OECD, subsequent years showed a weakening of the latter group's efforts towards collective action and norm setting in relation to development policy. The financial crisis led to far-reaching austerity measures and a strong pressure on development to prove its worth and "value for money". Discussions on the introduction of private sector logics under the label of results-based management took further root and represented development cooperation in a more predictable and controllable manner than was hitherto the case (see Holzapfel, 2016). In parallel, the development policies of OECD members became gradually more integrated into and part of foreign policy. This integration had two effects: first of all it promoted a more symptom-focused and crisis-oriented use of development funding, and secondly development policies began to formally express the pursuit of mutual interest as an objective. This is not to say that development policy had not been a foreign policy tool since the creation of the DAC in the 60s, but rather that—exceptions notwithstanding—it was new for the countries concerned to adopt policies explicitly stating that development funds should also be used to promote their own interests (Keijzer & Lundsgaarde, 2018).

This process of southernization has also been described as a return to policies and approaches that were dominant in previous decades, with 2000 to 2008 considered an exceptional period in the longer history of OECD development policy (Bergmann et al., 2019). Notwithstanding this perspective, recent years do show important European discursive and practice trends that suggest a more fundamental reorientation—with most OECD members, including the EU, stating a desire to move away from "donor–recipient relations" and "from aid to investment". Recent German development policy statements regularly feature these points of emphasis, while for Korea they have been a feature of its "bridge builder" identity as an OECD member throughout. As the next section discusses, ongoing changes in the EU's development policy provide important points of reference to both countries.

The Emergence of the Global Gateway Initiative

In April 2009, the European Commission published a policy proposal (a "Communication" in EU-speak) that proposed 28 measures to support developing countries in coping with the global economic financial crisis. One key measure concerned using ODA grants to "leverage" soft loans, which the EU expected would help developing countries finance critical infrastructure. Two years later, the European Commission's discourse in this area began to shift and spoke of the use of "innovative financial instruments, including under facilities for blending grants and loans" (EC [European Commission], 2011, p. 4) while emphasizing that this would not weaken its overarching poverty reduction objective.

At that time, dedicated trust funds and regional "platforms" had been set up and were promoting such blended finance, while remaining under the radar and not yet attracting much political attention. This changed in 2016 when the Commission proposed an "External Investment Plan" that brought together the regional platforms under a single roof with a stronger focus on promoting external investment and creating jobs—the latter linked to the EU's desire to address so-called root causes of migration to Europe (Lundsgaarde, 2017). During this same period, in 2016, the EU had adopted a Global Strategy on Foreign and Security Policy, which stated that the EU's development policy should become more flexible and aligned with its strategic interests. This followed and was followed by EU policy statements acknowledging the need to "differentiate" between different developing countries, with mutual interests being a legitimate focus of cooperation with "more advanced" developing countries (Bergmann et al., 2019).

A year after the External Investment Plan had been launched, EU ministers discussed elements for a Europe–Asia Connectivity Strategy, which sought to promote a "sustainable, comprehensive and rules-based approach to connectivity" (EC/EEAS, 2018). Following the European Parliament elections of 2019, the incoming European Commission leadership was lobbied to extend this regional strategy to one promoting connectivity in the world as a whole, thus competing with China's Belt and Road. The new leadership was lukewarm to the idea, while the Commission's Directorate General responsible for development policy advised against publishing the proposal (Bermingham, 2023). The document was thus prepared but not published, while the global pandemic meanwhile required attention to be focused on more immediate short-term measures. By the summer of 2021, EU foreign ministers nonetheless called for the development of an EU connectivity strategy that should be tabled by the spring of 2022 and should build on several existing strategies, including the EU's Asia–Pacific Strategy, as agreed by the ministers earlier that year (EC [European Council], 2021). In their statement, the ministers acknowledged that a "geostrategic approach to connectivity" would require both changing and combining the EU's economic, foreign, security and development policy objectives (EC, p. 2). In part because its proposal was already drafted, the Commission decided, however, to move faster and presented its Global Gateway Initiative much sooner, in December 2021 (EC/EEAS, 2021).

A key source of confusion (or debate) in the run-up to its publication was to what extent the strategy stressed the uniqueness of the EU's approach to infrastructure financing and its underlying value (stressing a "positive offer"), and to what extent the initiative sought to directly compete with China's BRI. While initial communication (including by the Commission President) emphasized the need to compete with China, the published proposal did not once mention the country. The question remained therefore whether the EU was seeking to beat China at its own game, or would provide a compelling alternative approach. The proposal was nonetheless clear in acknowledging the EU's own interests as a key driver:

> In assisting others, the EU will also be contributing to the promotion of its own interests, to strengthening the resilience of its supply chains, and to opening up more trade opportunities for the EU economy, in which approximately 38 million jobs are dependent on international trade. (EC/EEAS, 2021, p. 2)

As a consequence of the timing of its publication, the EU's proposal appeared at an inconvenient time in budgetary terms. The EU runs with seven-year multiannual financial frameworks that set the overall focus and limits of its annual budgets. The Global Gateway Initiative was announced at a time when the EU's external spending for 2021–2027 had already been prepared, including indicative budgets for 2021–2024. This, combined with Global Gateway's overarching target of mobilizing EUR 300 billion in external investment, attracted considerable attention to the question of whether the initiative would generate new investment or was just another way of presenting and communicating already ongoing activities. This setting may explain why, despite frequent appearances in speeches, more than a year passed before the initiative took further shape. Some ongoing projects were soon associated with Global Gateway, such as prominent investment in vaccine production facilities in various African countries. The summit between the African Union and the EU in February 2022 saw the announcement of a general Global Gateway Investment Package that would seek to meet half the EUR 300 billion investment target. The start of Russia's war against Ukraine a few days later, however, would absorb much of the EU's political priorities during subsequent months, although in June 2022 the G7 did adopt its Partnership on Global Infrastructure and Investment, with an overall USD 600 billion target—with the EU thus contributing to the realization of half this target.[2] In subsequent months, Global Gateway regularly featured in the EU's political discourse, yet there was little new information to convey.[3]

This lack of progress in Global Gateway changed in the run-up to the first meeting of EU foreign ministers as members of the Global Gateway Board on 11 December 2022. Interventions made by the ministers during this meeting contributed to the selection of flagship projects where quick results could be expected, which in turn led to the publication of basic information on these projects in early 2023. Although the proposal explained which instruments and resources would be made available, including up to EUR 18 billion in ODA grants, the increasing emphasis on flagship projects from late 2022 onwards raised confusion as to whether the initiative was principally about investment or (development) projects. Later in 2023, two key advisory groups were also created, namely a Business Advisory Group and a Civil Society and Local Authorities Dialogue Platform. The latter platform first met on 25 October 2023, a day before the first Global Gateway Forum was convened that attracted heads of state and other high-level officials from the EU and

[2] More information on the G7 Partnership can be found here: https://www.mofa.go.jp/files/100506918.pdf.

[3] Basic information on Global Gateway and the projects associated to the initiative can be found on the European Commission Global Gateway website: https://commission.europa.eu/strategy-and-policy/priorities-2019-2024/stronger-europe-world/global-gateway_en.

its partner countries to Brussels. This forum was held a week after China convened its third Belt and Road Forum for International Cooperation, the timing once more underlying the suggestion of competition between the two policy frameworks. Rather than reporting on the progress made towards the EU's overarching investment target, the Commission President instead emphasized that the EU had committed EUR 66 billion to the various projects, adding that almost half of this amount would be in the form of grants—a considerably higher amount than the EU 18 billion initially highlighted in the proposal (Von der Leyen, 2023).

Notwithstanding this discussion on the financing of Global Gateway, the associated "input confusion" and its slow and unconvincing start, the initiative's effect on the EU's long-term policy orientation and its external perception should not be underestimated. First of all, the frequent mention of the initiative by the leadership of the European Commission should be acknowledged, given that development policy has typically been a low salience topic for the EU for a long time. The renaming of the development policy portfolio to "international partnerships" by the Commission leadership in December 2019 was already pointing towards this reorientation. Since the policy proposal was published, few speeches by European Commissioners on international cooperation have failed to mention Global Gateway, while the initiative was also given considerable attention in the summits with the African Union (2022) and Latin America and the Caribbean (2023).

Conclusion: Implications for Germany and Korea

The Global Gateway initiative sets itself apart from earlier EU policy initiatives through the stronger integration with broader foreign and commercial policy interests, while also explicitly setting out the "domestic" economic interests that the country should promote. Paradoxically, while seen as a case of "southernization" this explicit focus on own interests in fact sets it apart from southern cooperation actors—notably China and its Belt and Road Initiative—where such interests are not articulated but instead merely implied. This difference may in part be explained by the aforementioned influence of results-based management and the accompanying austerity-driven policy debates in OECD members on specifying the concrete results and benefits of the use public funding.

The use of ODA more specifically also necessitates a strong focus on scrutinizing all objectives—i.e. in this case not the developing country benefits alone but also the EU's so-called return on investment.

Korea and Germany stand out from other DAC members in being known for having developed strong competencies in terms of cooperation with the private sector and in promoting investment more generally, in the case of Korea within the wider Asian region and, for Germany, through its G20 Compact with Africa initiative.[4] Typically these have been of either a thematic or regional focus, as opposed to being motivated by a global connectivity perspective such as with the EU and Chinese initiatives. Both Germany and Korea also face the challenge of considerable institutional fragmentation of their development cooperation systems, with both the EU and Chinese initiatives being more top-down driven initiatives. A related policy consideration is to what extent Korea and Germany would welcome a stronger focus on infrastructure investment in their bilateral cooperation portfolio, given that they additionally have multilateral actors (and in Germany's case: the EU) at their disposal.

In the event that similar such high-level infrastructure initiatives with an explicit "mutual benefit" motivation would be considered by either Germany or Korea, then it should be acknowledged that such initiatives will also have a strong influence on accountability patterns and societal debate as to the objectives and expected results of development policy. Such initiatives should thus be designed in close dialogue with different development policy stakeholders within Korean and German societies, so as not to unintentionally widen the gap between the public perception and actual practice of development cooperation. It is this underlying societal and political support that sets such initiatives apart from investment initiatives managed by SSC providers that OECD members may claim (not) to compete with. Such broad-based support is also needed, as effective and lasting investment in infrastructure takes considerable time to plan and conclude, which is why care should be taken to avoid such initiatives being associated with specific (coalitions of) political actors.

[4] For more information on the Compact with Africa, refer to: https://www.compactwithafrica.org/content/compactwithafrica/home.html.

References

Bergmann, J., Delputte, S., Keijzer, N., & Verschaeve, J. (2019). The evolution of the EU's development policy: Turning full circle. *European Foreign Affairs Review, 24*(4), 533–554.

Bermingham, F. (2023, October 24). 4 lost years: How the EU fumbled its response to China's belt and road with Global Gateway strategy. *South China Morning Post*. https://www.scmp.com/news/china/diplomacy/article/3238880/4-lost-years-how-eu-fumbled-its-response-chinas-belt-and-road

Borrell, J. (2020). *The Coronavirus pandemic and the new world it is creating*. https://www.eeas.europa.eu/eeas/coronavirus-pandemic-and-new-world-it-creating_en

European Council (EC) (2009). *Supporting developing countries in coping with the crisis*. https://eur-lex.europa.eu/LexUriServ/LexUriServ.do?uri=CELEX:52009DC0160:EN:HTML

EC. (2011). *Increasing the impact of EU development policy: An agenda for change*. https://eur-lex.europa.eu/legal-content/en/ALL/?uri=CELEX:52011DC0637

EC. (2021, July 12). A globally connected Europe—Council conclusions. https://data.consilium.europa.eu/doc/document/ST-10629-2021-INIT/en/pdf

EC and European External Action Service (EEAS). (2018). *Connecting Europe and Asia—Building blocks for an EU Strategy*. https://www.eeas.europa.eu/sites/default/files/joint_communication_-_connecting_europe_and_asia_-_building_blocks_for_an_eu_strategy_2018-09-19.pdf

EC and EEAS. (2021). *The Global Gateway*. https://eur-lex.europa.eu/legal-content/EN/TXT/?uri=CELEX%3A52021JC0030

Eyben, R., & Savage, L. (2013). Emerging and submerging powers: Imagined geographies in the new development partnership at the Busan Fourth High Level Forum. *Journal of Development Studies, 49*(4), 457–469. https://doi.org/10.1080/00220388.2012.733372

Holzapfel, S. (2016). Boosting or hindering aid effectiveness? An assessment of systems for measuring donor agency results. *Public Administration and Development, 36*, 3–19. https://doi.org/10.1002/pad.1749

Ito, S. (2023). *The "Easternization" of development: The politics of East Asia's developmentalist cooperatio*. Practical Action Publishing.

Keijzer, N., & Lundsgaarde, E. (2018). When "unintended effects" reveal hidden intentions: Implications of "mutual benefit" discourses for evaluating development cooperation. *Evaluation and Program Planning, 68*, 210–217.

Lundsgaarde, E. (2017). *The European fund for sustainable development: Changing the game?* (DIE Discussion Paper 29). German Development Institute/Deutsches Institut für Entwicklungspolitik (DIE).

Mawdsley, E. (2018). The "Southernisation" of development? *Asia Pacific Viewpoint, 59*, 173–185. https://doi.org/10.1111/apv.12192

OECD/DAC. (1996). *Shaping the 21st century: The contribution of development co-operation*. https://www.oecd.org/dac/2508761.pdf

Von der Leyen, U. (2021). *State of the Union Address 2021*. European Commission. https://state-of-the-union.ec.europa.eu/system/files/2022-12/soteu_2021_address_en.pdf

Von der Leyen, U. (2023, October 25). *Opening speech by President von der Leyen at the Global Gateway Forum*. https://ec.europa.eu/commission/presscorner/detail/en/speech_23_5305

CHAPTER 8

Multilateralism and Climate Justice

Songhee Han, Minah Kang, and Jale Tosun

Abstract This chapter investigates the climate justice principles and the mandate and scope of multilateral institutions in pursuit of sustainable and climate-resilient development. Specifically, the climate change operational framework and strategies of key multilateral development banks are analysed from the perspective of climate justice, along with implications for policymakers and practitioners and cases from the Republic of Korea (hereafter referred to as Korea) and Germany. This study sheds new light on the potential for multilateral climate governance to advance climate justice.

Keywords Climate justice · Just transition · Multilateral development banks · Climate finance · International development

S. Han (✉) · M. Kang
Ewha Womans University, Seoul, Republic of Korea
e-mail: songhee.han@ewha.ac.kr

M. Kang
e-mail: minahkang@ewha.ac.kr

J. Tosun
Heidelberg University, Heidelberg, Germany
e-mail: jale.tosun@ipw.uni-heidelberg.de

S. Klingebiel et al. (eds.), *Emerging Trends in International Development and Climate Policy*,
https://doi.org/10.1007/978-3-031-65671-2_8

Introduction

The rising severity of climate change requires more active and cooperative climate actions. Unfortunately, negative impacts of climate change disproportionately affect developing countries which have contributed little and have less capability to respond. On the other hand, developed countries, such as Germany and Korea, have polluted considerably in the past and already achieved rapid economic growth (Gutierrez et al., 2014; Hallegatte et al., 2016; Mendelsohn et al., 2006; Mirza, 2003; Tan et al., 2021; Ward & Shively, 2012). For instance, Germany, despite being a leader in renewable energy adoption and low-carbon transition in recent years, has a historical legacy of heavy industrialization that contributed to greenhouse gas emissions. Similarly, Korea has implemented ambitious climate policies and invested in climate technology to address its historical emissions caused by rapid industrialization and economic development. A recent study also warned of a "doom loop" phenomenon, which means the increasing frequency and magnitude of climate-induced disasters and the rising costs of disaster recovery will result in a lack of resources for proactive climate actions. This in turn leads to a vicious cycle of failure to address the causes of disasters (Laybourn et al., 2023). The fact that the climate crisis is more devastating to vulnerable countries and communities increases the need and urgency to analyse the current status and plan for a better future from a climate justice perspective.

These disparities between developed and developing nations in the environmental domain were codified in the United Nations Framework Convention on Climate Change (UNFCCC) (UN [United Nations], 1992) as the principle of "common but differentiated responsibilities". Since then, there have been various discussions on, and efforts to climate finance and climate technology transfer from developed to developing countries in consideration of historical responsibility. However, neither the actual needs nor the promised targets for addressing climate change are being met. For example, the goal of mobilizing USD 100 billion in climate finance by 2020, which was pledged at the 15th Conference of the Parties (COP) in 2009 under the UNFCCC, was extended to 2025 at COP21 in 2015. As of 2020, USD 83.3 billion was confirmed to have been raised (OECD, 2022), but achieving the climate financing target will be challenging as countries also increase their domestic carbon neutral investments.

Climate change poses a global challenge that calls for a multilateral response. A country cannot address climate issues by itself. Every nation has a responsibility to take part in climate actions since climate is global commons. In this regard, multilateral institutions are one of the important agents in combating climate change. This chapter will analyse climate actions of multilateral development banks from the perspective of climate justice. Specifically, climate action plans of the World Bank Group, the Asian Development Bank and the European Bank for Reconstruction and Development will be examined, including cases from Korea and Germany.

Multilateral Activities and Climate Justice

The notion of climate justice places significant emphasis on climate change as a matter of ethics and politics, with a particular focus on the interplay of environmental accountability, human rights and social justice (Baxi, 2016; Caney, 2020; Mary Robinson Foundation, 2018; Robinson & Shine, 2018). It examines the issue of climate change's unequal effects on marginalized communities, emphasizing the importance of finding solutions for the rights and inclusion of those who are most impacted, particularly in developing countries. The primary elements encompass the obligation of developed countries with regard to historical emissions, the imperative of ensuring equitable transitions for workers in fossil fuel sectors, the pursuit of legal measures to establish accountability, and the incorporation of community-driven adaptation initiatives. Climate justice aims to adopt a comprehensive approach that promotes sustainable development while also guaranteeing fairness and equity in addressing climate-related issues.

In the pursuit of low-carbon and sustainable development, there is a growing need to more deliberately and comprehensively integrate climate justice principles that recognize the ethical consequences of climate change and the actions taken to mitigate its effects, while also considering their broader implications for justice, into development cooperation and climate actions. However, there have not been many studies exploring this critical subject, particularly concerning the role played by multilateral development banks (MDBs), who play a crucial role in allocating substantial financial resources towards the mitigation and adaptation of climate change. Additionally, they provide expertise and guidance to assist nations in formulating and executing climate-friendly policies, while also facilitating the attraction of private sector investments in climate-related projects. Furthermore, MDBs may support research and innovation endeavours aimed at addressing climate change mitigation and adaptation.

For instance, Lee et al. (2023) investigated the performance of MDBs and asked what the ideal characteristics were for development and climate banks. Their analysis included benefits and constraints of MDB operations in four aspects: financial models; finance instruments for governments; finance instruments for the private sector and mobilization; and goals, impact measurement and reporting. As an agenda for change, they suggested nine topics, which included predictable and sustained MDB support for a country's climate and development strategy, helping countries borrow from markets on better terms, consolidation of MDB concessional climate finance to support larger country portfolios of climate lending, and assessing impact for an integrated climate and development mission.

Getzel and Prizzon (2023) acknowledged MDBs as the largest contributor of climate finance to low- and middle-income countries, and recommended ways in which MDBs could more effectively operate in achieving climate goals. Specifically, they emphasized that MDBs need a more robust integration of climate and development strategies, MDBs can scale up climate finance, and MDBs must create more effective incentives for client countries. For each topic, they examined the challenges that MDBs face in delivering climate interventions and that shareholders and MDB management can do and should prioritize.

Both reports recognized the significant contributions and important roles of MDBs in supporting climate actions of countries. Developing more predictable, sustained and robust strategies for integrating development and climate was one of the commonly suggested future actions, along with enlarging the amount of funding for climate solutions. However, neither of the two reports puts much emphasis on climate justice. They did not directly mention what climate justice is, nor clearly specify why and how climate justice principle needs to be considered and can be reflected in the effective operation of MDBs.

Climate Justice in the Strategies of Multilateral Development Banks

The strategies of three key multilateral development banks (MDBs) will be investigated in this section from climate justice perspective, which are the World Bank Group, the Asian Development Bank and the European Bank for Reconstruction and Development. MDBs jointly publish an annual report on their climate finance, and according to the report, these three institutions take a large portion of the total (Table 8.1).

World Bank Group

The World Bank Group (WBG) consists of five institutions: the International Bank for Reconstruction and Development (IBRD), the International Development Association (IDA), the International Finance Corporation (IFC), the Multilateral Investment Guarantee Agency (MIGA) and the International Centre for Settlement of Investment Disputes (ICSID). Germany, the fourth-largest shareholder in the WBG, has been a member of IBRD since 1952, of IDA since 1960, IFC since 1956, MIGA since 1988 and ICSID since 1969. It strongly supports green, resilient and inclusive development. Korea initially joined as a beneficiary of IBRD in 1955 and of IDA in 1961. However, it successfully graduated from IDA in 1973 and IBRD in 1955. It became a member of IFC in 1962

Table 8.1 Climate finance commitments targeting low- and middle-income countries (USD billion, percentage of the total amount)

MDBs	*2019*	*2020*	*2021*	*2022*
World Bank Group	18.4 (44.3%)	21.3 (56.1%)	28.0 (55.2%)	31.7 (52.2%)
Asian Development Bank	7.1 (17.1%)	5.3 (13.9%)	4.8 (9.5%)	7.1 (11.7%)
European Bank for Reconstruction and Development	3.9 (9.4%)	2.3 (6.1%)	4.8 (9.5%)	4.3 (7.1%)
Sum of the three MDBs above	29.4 (70.8%)	28.9 (76.1%)	37.6 (74.2%)	43.1 (71.0%)
Total amount of commitment by all MDBs	41.5 (100%)	38.0 (100%)	50.7 (100%)	60.7 (100%)

Source Adapted from European Investment Bank (2023)

and MIGA in 1988. Since 2013, Korea has been operating a WBG office focusing on disruptive digital innovation and innovative green growth.

The WBG published its five-year Climate Change Action Plan (CCAP) in 2016, around the time when the Paris Agreement was drafted and signed. The WBG recognized the adverse effect of climate change on development and the disproportional impact of climate risks on vulnerable countries, and adopted a CCAP to accelerate member countries' climate action. The four priorities of the CCAP were to support transformational policies and institutions, leverage resources, scale up climate action and align internal processes and work with others. With the CCAP 2016–2020, the WBG increased financial and technical support to countries and is now known as the largest multilateral climate finance provider to developing countries. In the second CCAP, the WBG states that it pursues Green, Resilient and Inclusive Development approach, emphasizing integration of climate and development. Their main efforts in the CCAP 2021–2025 are categorized as aligning climate and development, prioritizing key systems transitions and financing to support the transitions.

Both in the first and second CCAP, the term climate justice itself is not mentioned directly. However, both the two CCAPs addressed the concept of climate justice from the introduction. For instance, the CCAP 2016–2020 mentioned "Lower-income countries suffer disproportionately from natural disasters, with almost half of disaster casualties occurring in low-income countries, and economic losses sometimes exceeding 10% of gross domestic product (GDP) in small, vulnerable economies". The CCAP 2021–2025 says "The World Bank Group (WBG) recognizes that globally, the poor, who are the least responsible for greenhouse gas (GHG) emissions, often suffer the most from climate change impacts". Just transition from coal is also highlighted in the second CCAP. These signify that the WBG considers climate justice principles when establishing its CCAPs.

In addition to recognizing the principles of climate justice, aligning climate and development is essential because climate action should be harmonized with broader development objectives. In the initial CCAP, the WBG committed to supporting client countries in integrating the development and climate agendas with a focus on the poorest and most vulnerable. Building on this commitment, the WBG indicates in the subsequent CCAP that it will engage at the country level in climate and development diagnostics, planning, and policies; align its financing flow with the Paris Agreement; and increase climate finance for both mitigation and adaptation to maximize the impact.

As a strategic approach to climate action, the WBG has selected and focused on several main areas. In the first phase of the CCAP, six high-impact areas were identified, which are renewable energy and energy efficiency; sustainable mobility; sustainable and resilient cities; climate-smart land use, water and food security; green competitiveness; and leaving no one behind. The second phase targeted five key systems: energy; agriculture, food, water and land; cities; transport; and manufacturing. These five were chosen since they collectively contribute to over 90% of global greenhouse gas emissions.

To implement its CCAPs, the WBG has actually augmented its climate finance allocations, particularly for low- and middle-income countries. In addition, the second CCAP explicitly indicated that the WBG's commitment was increasing the percentage of climate finance from 20% of lending in 2016 to 28% by 2020, and this target has been surpassed every year since 2018. The share of the WBG projects incorporating climate finance also enlarged from 26% in 2015 to 62% in 2020. This substantial increase reflects the WBG's dedication to climate-related initiatives.

Asian Development Bank

Asian Development Bank (ADB) directed its attention to the Asia and Pacific region, which "has the largest number of climate-vulnerable people worldwide, women being among the most vulnerable" (ADB, 2017). Both Korea and Germany, as founding members of ADB, actively contribute to the climate fund. As an example, Korea has committed to the Future Carbon Fund, while Germany has pledged support to the Asia–Pacific Climate Finance Fund and the Energy Transition Mechanism Partnership Trust Fund.

ADB's strategic document for climate response is Climate Change Operational Framework 2017–2030 (CCOF2030). The CCOF2030 is formulated to facilitate low greenhouse gas emissions and climate-resilient development in the Asia and Pacific. Through this, ADB endeavours to position itself as a leading development partner of its member countries and to reinforce its climate operations. For monitoring and reporting of the CCOF2030, a results framework is presented, with 45 performance indicators. Implementation will be conducted in two phases: (i) current and near-term operations, from 2017 to 2023 and (ii) long-term operations, from 2024 to 2030.

While the term “climate justice” is not explicitly stated in the CCOF2030, ADB acknowledges the disproportional impact of climate change in the Asia and Pacific region, the heterogeneity of member countries, including small island and low-lying countries, and the heightened vulnerability of specific individuals or groups, such as women and the poorest populations, in terms of climate challenges. It can be inferred that climate justice principles are considered when the CCOF2030 is designed. Additionally, “just transition” is not found in the CCOF2030, however, ADB was one of the MDBs that jointly committed to supporting a just transition (ADB, 2021).

There are five principles of the CCOF2030: (i) supporting ambitious climate objectives articulated in nationally determined contributions and other climate plans; (ii) accelerating low greenhouse gas emissions development; (iii) promoting climate change adaptation; (iv) integrating climate change adaptation and disaster risk management; (v) linking climate actions to wider sustainable development agenda. The first principle shows ADB’s commitments to promote coherence and integration between climate and development objectives. To ensure this, ADB institutionally strives to mainstream climate considerations into its strategies, policies, plans and projects, while at the same time, actively supporting member countries in translating climate action into their national policy frameworks.

To effectively monitor and evaluate ADB’s performance, a report to review the CCOF2030 results framework in the middle of the first implementation phase was released. Alignment of the CCOF2030 with relevant documents or indicators, including ADB’s Strategy 2030 Operational Priority 3, ADB Corporate Results Framework 2019–2024, Sustainable Development Goals, the Paris Agreement, and Sendai Framework for Disaster Risk Reduction 2015–2030, was also examined. Regarding the amount of climate finance, ADB sets a target of USD 6 billion by 2020. According to ADB Annual Report 2020, ADB disbursed USD 4.3 billion in 2020 and USD 10.8 billion cumulatively for 2019 and 2020. Recently, USD 6.7 billion was provided through ADB in 2022, contributing to a cumulative total of USD 21 billion for the period 2019 to 2022. ADB has continuously scaled up climate finance and monitored its operations for better measures against climate change.

European Bank for Reconstruction and Development

Founded in 1991, the European Bank for Reconstruction and Development (EBRD) has been committed to green investment and assessing the environmental and social impacts of all of its projects from the beginning. Germany has been one of the main sources of foreign direct investment in the EBRD's countries of operation, and a driving force behind the bank's approach to financing low-carbon transition. Korea has acted as an EBRD donor since 1993 and is an important contributor to the bank's work, including in the field of green growth and climate change.

With regard to climate change, the EBRD carries out climate risk assessments and integrates adaptation measures in its investment operations. In 2020, the EBRD adopted the Green Economy Transition (GET) approach for the period 2021 to 2025 in order to accelerate the transition to a low-carbon and resilient economies in its countries of operations. Through the GET approach, the EBRD will increase green financing to more than 50% of its annual business volume by 2025 as well as aim to reach net annual greenhouse gas emissions reductions of at least 25 million tonnes over the five-year period.

To achieve these goals, the GET approach (i) assesses projects in relation to the principles of the Paris Agreement; (ii) enhances policy engagement for the development of long-term low-carbon strategies and greening of financial systems; and (iii) scales investments across a set of priority environmental, climate mitigation and resilience themes, which includes just transition. Regarding just transition, the GET approach acknowledges the need to provide sustainable economic and job alternatives to communities reliant on sectors due to decline in a low-carbon future. More generally, the EBRD states in the GET approach that for just transition it is necessary that the benefits of transition are shared widely, including by those who stand to lose economically, thus recognizing the importance of considering the distribution of costs and benefits of a green economy transition. Korea, for example, has stressed that the EBRD should concentrate on establishing efficient and green energy systems in order to mitigate supply shocks that may threaten reaching the long-term goal of carbon neutrality (EBRD, n.d.). Germany's position on just transition aligns with that of the bank and has not been subject to country-specific reflections or interpretations.

The GET approach also acknowledges the need to integrate climate finance policies with social policies; social policies should provide job alternatives to communities, depending on sectors that are likely to decline as the transformation towards a low-carbon economy advances.

Areas the EBRD has identified as requiring enhanced attention in relation to just transition are energy systems, the decarbonization of industries, and issues related to cities and the environmental infrastructure. Loans, equity and guarantees are the main direct forms of financing the EBRD uses to achieve the goals put forth by the GET approach. The EBRD is committed to international cooperation, which includes the EU, the Climate Investment Funds, the Green Climate Fund and the Global Environment Facility.

Challenges, Opportunities, and Recommendations for Multilateral Climate Justice

This chapter has examined the strategies implemented by major multilateral development banks to facilitate a just transition to address the negative impacts of climate change. These institutions utilize their array of pre-existing financial tools to provide green financing but also to enhance the connection between climate finance policy and climate justice. The World Bank Group (WBG), the Asian Development Bank (ADB) and the European Bank for Reconstruction and Development (EBRD) have made contributions to climate justice by adopting climate action strategies that prioritize ethical and social considerations.

Multilateral development banks (MDBs) can play a crucial role in this process by ensuring that climate action is both environmentally efficient and socially just, by addressing the needs of the most vulnerable groups, and distributing the responsibilities and advantages of climate action fairly across the global community. MDBs have the capacity to tackle both domestic and global inequities in the impacts of climate change. By possessing this dual competence, they are positioned as a significant force in promoting a fair and impartial approach to addressing the complex difficulties presented by climate change.

Although there have been encouraging advancements and the possibility for even greater effects, there remain substantial obstacles in properly executing climate justice concepts. Although progress has been achieved, there is still a requirement for ongoing dedication and ingenuity in incorporating climate justice into the worldwide efforts to address climate change.

It is clear that there is a requirement for a more intentional and thorough incorporation of climate justice ideas into development cooperation and climate efforts. Proficiency in this integration necessitates a profound comprehension of the ethical ramifications of climate change and the measures implemented to alleviate its consequences. In order to ensure that the benefits and burdens of climate action are distributed fairly among all nations, especially taking into account the interests and rights of the most vulnerable countries and communities, it is imperative that their actions and plans demonstrate a strong dedication to sustainable development, equity and fairness.

For instance, as important contributors and influential decision makers in MDBs, both Germany and Korea have made strides in incorporating climate justice principles into climate actions. However, there is room for increased impact. This could involve augmenting the volume of climate finance, and establishing innovative mechanisms for climate funds or investments, specifically geared towards promoting climate justice. In addition, Germany and Korea can more actively support climate technology development and transfer. This includes more proactive engagement in capacity building initiatives and policy consulting tailored to the needs of domestic and global vulnerable groups. By leveraging expertise and resources of Germany and Korea, both countries can further contribute to bridging the technological and knowledge gaps and advancing climate justice on a global scale through MDBs.

In conclusion, both the strategies of MDBs and a concerted effort by member countries such as Germany and Korea to amplify their commitments within MDBs are pivotal. By reinforcing their dedication to sustainable development, equity and fairness, MDBs can serve as catalysts for a more just and inclusive approach to addressing the challenges posed by climate change on a global scale and ensuring a more equitable and resilient future for all.

References

Asian Development Bank. (2017). *Climate Change Operational Framework 2017–2030: Enhanced actions for low greenhouse gas emissions and climate-resilient development*. https://www.adb.org/documents/climate-change-operational-framework-2017-2030

Asian Development Bank. (2021). *ADB joins MDBs to support just transition toward net-zero economies*. https://www.adb.org/news/adb-joins-mdbs-support-just-transition-toward-net-zero-economies

Baxi, U. (2016). Towards a climate change justice theory? *Journal of Human Rights and the Environment, 7*(1), 7–31.

Caney, S. (2020). Climate justice. *Stanford Encyclopedia of Philosophy*. https://plato.stanford.edu/entries/justice-climate/

European Bank for Reconstruction and Development (EBRD). (n.d.). *Governor statement: Republic of Korea, In-chang Song, temporary alternate governor*. https://www.ebrd.com/documents/osg/speech-korea-e.pdf

EBRD (European Bank for Reconstruction and Development). (2020). *Green economy transition approach 2021–2025*. https://www.ebrd.com/documents/comms-and-bis/get-20212025.pdf

European Investment Bank (2023). *2022 Joint report on multilateral development banks' climate finance*. https://www.eib.org/en/publications/20230128-2022-joint-report-on-multilateral-development-banks-climate-finance

Getzel, B., & Prizzon, A. (2023). *Climate-smart reform of multilateral development banks* (ODI Policy Brief). ODI. (https://odi.org/en/publications/climate-smart-reform-of-multilateraldevelopment-banks-priorities-for-the-g20).

Gutierrez, M., McFarland, W., & Fonua, L. (2014). *Zero poverty... think again. Impact of climate change on development efforts*. ODI. https://odi.org/en/publications/zero-poverty-think-again-the-impact-of-climate-change-on-development-efforts/

Hallegatte, S., Bangalore, M., Bonzanigo, L., Fay, M., Kane, T., Narloch, U., Rozenberg, J., Treguer, D., & Vogt-Schilb, A. (2016). *Shock waves: Managing the impacts of climate change on poverty* (Climate Change and Development Series). World Bank.

Laybourn, L., Throp, H., & Sherman, S. (2023). *1.5°C—Dead or alive? The risks to transformational change from reaching and breaching the Paris Agreement goal. IPPR and Chatham House*. IPPR. https://www.ippr.org/articles/1-5c-dead-or-alive

Lee, N., Laxton, V., & Matthews, S. (2023). *What would the ideal development and climate MDB look like?* (CGD Policy Paper 299). Center for Global Development.

Mary Robinson Foundation. (2018). *Principles of climate justice*. http://www.mrfcj.org/principles-of-climate-justice

Mendelsohn, R., Dinar, A., & Williams, L. (2006). The distributional impact of climate change on rich and poor countries. *Environment and Development Economics, 11*(2), 159–178.

Mirza, M. (2003). Climate change and extreme weather events: Can developing countries adapt? *Climate Policy, 3*(3), 233–248.

OECD. (2022). *Climate finance provided and mobilised by developed countries in 2016–2020: Insights from disaggregated analysis, climate finance and the USD 100 billion goal.* OECD Publishing.

Robinson, M., & Shine, T. (2018). Achieving a climate justice pathway to 1.5 °C. *Nature Climate Change, 8*, 564–569.

Tan, X., Zhu, K., Meng, X., Gu, B., Wang, Y., Meng, F., Liu, G., & Li, H. (2021). Research on the status and priority needs of developing countries to address climate change. *Journal of Cleaner Production, 289*. https://doi.org/10.1016/j.jclepro.2020.125669

United Nations. (1992). *United Nations Framework Convention on Climate Change.* https://treaties.un.org/Pages/ViewDetailsIII.aspx?src=TREATY&mtdsg_no=XXVII-7&chapter=27&Temp=mtdsg3&clang=_en

Ward, P., & Shively, G. (2012). Vulnerability, income growth and climate change. *World Development, 40*(5), 916–927.

World Bank Group (WBG). (2016). *Climate change action plan 2016–2020.* https://thedocs.worldbank.org/en/doc/677331460056382875-0020022016/original/WBGClimateChangeActionPlanpublicversion.pdf

World Bank Group (WBG). (2021). *World Bank Group climate change action plan 2021–2025: Supporting green, resilient, and inclusive development.* World Bank Group. https://openknowledge.worldbank.org/entities/publication/ee8a5cd7-ed72-542d-918b-d72e07f96c79

PART III

Exploring Collaborations and New Actor Constellations

CHAPTER 9

A Comparative Analysis of the Climate Change Mitigation Efforts of Korea and Germany: Implemented Technology and Financial Mechanism Projects Under the UNFCCC

Tae Kun Kim, Jee Hyo Jeon, and Donmin Lee

Abstract While technology aids the fight against climate change, this chapter focuses on contrasting Korea and Germany's approaches, not just strategies, in utilizing technology for achieving green transitions,

T. K. Kim (✉) · D. Lee
Center for Strategic Planning, National Institute of Green Technology (NIGT), Seoul, Korea
e-mail: taekun@nigt.re.kr

D. Lee
e-mail: donmin@nigt.re.kr

J. H. Jeon
Department of Sociology, Ewha Womans University, Seoul, Korea

S. Klingebiel et al. (eds.), *Emerging Trends in International Development and Climate Policy*,
https://doi.org/10.1007/978-3-031-65671-2_9

carbon neutrality and climate responses. Funded by Technology Mechanism (TM) and Green Climate Fund (GCF), Korea prioritizes smaller scale TM-backed technical assistance and domestic infrastructure, while Germany focuses on larger, GCF-financed international projects. This offers valuable insights into complementary national approaches to leverage technology collaboration for effective climate action.

Keywords Korea · Germany · Climate change · Technology mechanism · Financial mechanism

Introduction

South Korea's efforts to address climate change have been in full swing since 2009, when it launched a national policy for low-carbon green growth, leading to the declaration of carbon neutrality by 2050 in 2020, and the establishment and implementation of domestic policies and systems along with the proposal of national emission reduction targets (three in total, with the latest version submitted in 2021). Despite these efforts, actual results have been lacklustre, with the share of renewable energy in South Korea's energy mix currently at 8.1% (as of 2022) and greenhouse gas (GHG) emissions at 676.6 million tonnes (as of 2021) (Ministry of Environment, n.d.).

South Korea's response to the climate crisis is characterized by its prioritization of green technologies (which can be substituted for climate technologies in the context of this article) as a key enabler to achieve its mitigation targets and its continued strengthening of investment and support for international development cooperation (ODA Korea, 2023).

South Korea's situation can be understood as an appropriate environment to explore technology-oriented cooperation with Germany to combat climate change. Both countries have a proactive stance on climate change, have increased their investment in international development cooperation projects, and have capabilities as technological powerhouses, which could lead to meaningful synergies through mutual cooperation in addressing the climate crisis. In particular, technology is recognized as a tool that has the potential to solve 70% of the climate crisis response problem (United Nations, 2023).

Technical cooperation requires investment. In particular, exploring technical cooperation through a financial support framework such as the Green Climate Fund, which is a representative source of funding for technical cooperation in response to climate change, would be a stable form of cooperation.

Against this backdrop, this chapter sets the macro-objective of promoting technical cooperation to respond to the climate crisis in Korea and Germany, and draws implications for the planning and implementation of meaningful joint climate technical cooperation projects in the future through a comparative analysis of the technical assistance projects carried out by both countries under the UNFCCC.

Method and Results

The methods utilized in this chapter are as follows. First, we make a comparison of the basic national goals of the two countries to address climate change, the key contents of these goals, and their characteristics in the field of international cooperation. Second, we outline the history of the bilateral external activities to address climate change conducted by the two countries since the Paris Agreement in order to examine their willingness and methods to cooperate in addressing the climate crisis. Third, we examine and analyse the activities of the two countries in the technical and financial mechanisms of the United Nations Framework Convention on Climate Change (UNFCCC) and their participation in individual projects under each mechanism to highlight differences in approach, specification of major project areas, and key outcomes achieved by each country. In doing so, we sought implications for complementary areas or approaches for bilateral cooperation.

In terms of the national targets and related highlights of the two countries' climate change response and international cooperation, Germany has, for decades, been proposing progressive emissions reduction targets in line with EU policies. Germany has set targets to reduce its emissions by 65% by 2030 and 88% by 2040 compared to 1990 levels, and to reach carbon neutrality by 2045, and is implementing a range of policies in line with these targets (Climate Action Tracker, 2023). South Korea has updated its nationally determined contribution (NDC) three times. The first NDC presented a 37% reduction target compared to business-as-usual (submitted in 2016), the second was a 28% reduction, with 2017 as the base year (submitted in 2020), and the update is aiming for a

40% reduction by 2018 (2021). To achieve this goal, the government is promoting a series of policies, including the enactment of the Basic Act on Carbon-neutral Green Growth (September 2021) and the establishment of the Basic Plan for Carbon-neutral Green Growth (March 2023). While both countries are similar in their urgency in setting targets and working towards reductions, there are differences in their approaches. In one of the most important areas, energy, South Korea is still heavily reliant on nuclear power and emphasizes going carbon free, while Germany's response is to phase out nuclear power and increase the proportion of renewable energy (Maennel & Kim, 2018). In terms of collaboration, it is worth looking at international development cooperation as a representative activity, independent of its contribution to the national target. Germany is among the top three providers of grant equivalents for international development cooperation, alongside the US and the UK. Korea has been steadily increasing its contribution, growing from USD 1.75 billion in 2013 to USD 2.81 billion in 2022, a 60.6% growth rate.

Our review of cooperation cases between the two countries starts in 2019 (Table 9.1), when, in South Korea, national policies for climate action after the Paris Agreement were being revised (Ministry of Environment, Korea, 2023), and in Germany Chancellor Angela Merkel's fourth term in office (November 2017–December 2021) had just begun. Each year, the two countries have strengthened cooperation in specific areas, including the signing of a joint declaration of intent for the establishment of an Energy Partnership to further strengthen and institutionalize the successful bilateral cooperation in the field of energy transition in 2019 and the roadmap that defines the framework for the future cooperation of the partnership in 2020, whereas both countries agreed to set up a high-level cooperation committee that meets at least once a year to discuss energy policy related issues as well as the means and results of cooperation.

Between late 2021 and early 2022, the leadership of both countries changed: Olaf Scholz became the new Chancellor of Germany in 2021, and Yoon Suk-yeol took office as the new President of South Korea in 2022. The two leaders have met twice, first on the sidelines of the United Nations General Assembly in New York in September 2022 and then in Seoul in May 2023. During the second meeting, Korea expressed its intent to join the Climate Club, an initiative by Chancellor Scholz aimed at accelerating climate action and encouraging steeper mitigation targets.

Table 9.1 Bilateral cooperation between Germany and Korea related to climate crisis (since 2019)

Bilateral	• Signed a joint declaration of intent for the establishment of an Energy Partnership (2019) • Signed the roadmap that defines the framework for the future cooperation of the partnership (2020) (Working Group on "Energy Transition", Working Group on "New Green Energy Technologies", Working Group on "Nuclear Decommissioning")

Source Energiepartnerschaft Deutschland—Korea, 2023

The activities of the two countries in the technical and financial mechanisms under the UNFCCC were analysed by focusing on their business history (Table 9.2). In the case of Korea, the Climate Technology Centre and Network (CTCN) and the Technical Executive Committee (TEC), which constitute the technology mechanism, have consistently been chaired by senior officials from the ministry in charge of NDE (Ministry of Science and ICT) and experts from the ministry's affiliated organizations, and Korea has the largest number of member organizations for technical assistance within the CTCN (99 out of 817). In addition, Korea has been successful in attracting a CTCN Coordinating Liaison Office in Korea to support enhanced cooperation with the GCF and strengthen technical cooperation in the Asia–Pacific region. (The agreement was signed in 2021, with the opening ceremony held in 2022.) Under this environment, three pro bono Technical Assistance (TA) projects supported by Korea have been regularized since 2022 in agreement with the CTCN. To date, Korea has participated in a total of 14 TA activities as a host and partner organization. The targets of the TA projects are divided by continent, with seven projects in Asia and six in Africa, and the same number of projects (six each) in mitigation and adaptation.

In the case of Germany, there are no examples of director activities in the CTCN, and private sector experts are active in the TEC. The total number of TA projects in Germany is small at four, but they range across Africa, Eastern Europe, Pacific Rim and the Caribbean, and capacity building efforts are observed through 14 publication activities.

Looking at the GCF projects that were hosted and active in Korea in 2013, Korea has two Accredited Entities and only one completed project, on energy efficiency in Indonesia. Germany has a total of two Accredited

Table 9.2 Activity comparison of Germany and Korea in technology and financial mechanisms

		Korea	*Germany*
Technology mechanism	Overview	• CTCN Liaison Office (Partnership and Liaison Office, PALO) hosted in Korea (2021) • Highest network members (99 of 817 are Korean) (CTCN, 2023)	Has the third-largest membership: • South Korea (99) • USA (49) • Germany (42) • UK (39) • France (36)
	Technical Assistance (TA)	• Initiated pro bono projects to enhance Korean network members' engagement in collaboration with CTCN (2022–) • 14 TA projects implemented	• 4 TA projects implemented and 14 publications
Financial mechanism	Overview	• Green Climate Fund hosted in Korea (2013) • Two accredited entities (KDB, KOICA)	• Two accredited entities (Deutsche Bank, GIZ)
	Green Climate Fund Project	• 1 project implemented	• 10 projects implemented • Projects in response to the needs of beneficiary countries on different continents conducted
Summarized		• Technology adaptation, financial access, and domestic institution utilization in the frame of Technology and Financial Mechanism via office provision and support projects promoted • More activity within the Technology Mechanism than the Financial Mechanism • CTCN technical support projects need to be enhanced qualitatively, and GCF projects need to be enhanced quantitatively and qualitatively	• More activity within the Financial Mechanism than the Technology Mechanism • Technology Mechanism contributions remain modest relative to country size and potential

Source Information for the "Technology mechanism" and "Financial mechanism" sections was sourced from the Climate Technology Centre and Network (2023) and Green Climate Fund (2023) websites. The author compiled the "Summarized" section based on the preceding text and this information

Entities (AEs) (as of November 2022), and a total of 10 projects have been implemented in various fields.

Conclusion and Discussion

Both countries are actively setting ambitious emission reduction targets and demonstrating urgency in tackling climate change, but Germany has consistently proposed stronger targets in line with EU policies, aiming for more significant reductions by 2030 and 2040 compared to South Korea. And Germany aims for complete reliance on renewable energy and has phased out nuclear power, while South Korea still heavily relies on nuclear power and focuses on achieving carbon neutrality, maintaining its nuclear programme. This difference shows contrasting policy stances on the role of nuclear energy in climate mitigation. In spite of the difference in key areas such as renewable energy and international cooperation. Germany's strong targets and leadership in international support are noteworthy, while South Korea's increasing ambition and potential to expand its international role deserve attention. By comparing and learning from each other, both countries can further refine their strategies and make more significant contributions to global climate action.

Reflecting on bilateral cooperation events in addressing climate crises jointly, two important implications can be extracted. First, we see strengthened bilateral cooperation. Joint research efforts in renewable energy, carbon capture and storage, offshore wind development, hydrogen, energy efficiency, and smart grids are tangible examples of progress. Furthermore, annual cooperation and hosting and collaborating on major climate events such as the G20 Climate Sustainability Working Group and the Clean Energy Ministerial demonstrate their ongoing commitment.

Secondly, the leadership in multilateral governance is underlined. By co-hosting events and showcasing successful bilateral cooperation, they suggest both countries see themselves as global leaders in climate action. By demonstrating successful bilateral cooperation, they may encourage other countries to follow suit. Especially, spearhead climate action demonstrates both global responsibility and a positive national image in multilateral relations.

However, there are some challenges and opportunities. Since the change in leadership, both countries have not engaged in significant collaboration at the national level, jeopardizing past joint achievements.

This lack of collaboration highlights the importance of continued collaboration. A key challenge is in maintaining political will; changes in government leadership could impact priorities and commitment to cooperation. Balancing national interests with joint climate goals can be challenging, and require ongoing compromise. To expand collaboration further, scaling up successful projects and exploring new avenues of cooperation can further accelerate progress for both countries.

Considering the project-focused activities of Korea and Germany in UNFCCC, both exhibit distinctive roles in supporting the UNFCCC's Technology and Financial Mechanisms. Korea leans towards the technical assistance side. It actively participates in the Climate Technology Centre and Network (CTCN) and Technical Executive Committee (TEC), evidenced by numerous projects and targets in the CTCN's programme. Its efforts attract organizations from both mechanisms and it promotes Korean-style pro bono projects. Germany however prioritizes financial support. It plays a leading role in the Green Climate Fund (GCF), boasting a significantly higher number and wider variety of funded projects compared to Korea. Pertaining to collaboration opportunities, while both countries demonstrate strong commitment to national mitigation targets and international cooperation, optimizing their partnership could yield greater benefits. Korea can, for example, partner with German implementers, enabling Korea to leverage German expertise and thereby maximize gains from technical assistance projects. Of course, Germany can engage in Korean-supported GCF projects, which would enhance its involvement in projects aligned with Korea's priorities. As an essential issue, linking the CTCN/TEC and GCF to facilitate integrated mitigation and adaptation projects remains challenging due to differing perspectives. Developing countries prioritize needs-driven, large-scale investment support, while developed countries favour a more nuanced, demand-driven approach.

Korea and Germany's active involvement in both mechanisms positions them as potential catalysts for a more synergistic approach, stressing Korea's strengths, such as infrastructure-focused approach and rapid decision-making culture, and utilizing Germany's strengths, such as demand-driven process and multifaceted cooperation activities. Generally, by combining their strengths, Korea and Germany can bridge the gap between developing and developed countries' perspectives. A more integrated approach could create a positive feedback loop, whereby developing countries' needs drive larger-scale investment support from the

GCF. And Korea and Germany's leadership can pave the way for a more effective and impactful global response to climate change.

The higher consumption of carbon-intensive power generation and production in Southeast Asia compared to the Western nations highlights the need for collaboration between Korea and Germany. This collaboration could establish an enabling framework for cooperation and serve as a model for other countries. Through joint projects utilizing the Technology and Financial Mechanism, Korea could leverage German expertise to strengthen its capabilities in developing sustainable and high-quality clean energy solutions. In turn, Germany can leverage Korea's well-established networks in Southeast Asia to expand its reach in promoting sustainable practices. This collaboration will undoubtedly contribute to motivating other countries to join the fight against climate change.

Acknowledgements This analysis work was supported by the National Institute of Green Technology grant funded by the Ministry of Science and ICT (No. C2320401).

References

Climate Action Tracker. (2023). *Germany*. https://climateactiontracker.org/countries/germany/targets/. Accessed 29 August 2023.

Climate Technology Centre & Network (CTCN). (2023). *Technical assistance*. https://www.ctc-n.org/technical-assistance. Accessed 15 May 2023.

Energiepartnerschaft Deutschland-Korea. (2023). *The Korean-German Energy Partnership (한-독 에너지 파트너십)*. https://www.energypartnership-korea.org/home/. Accessed 15 August 2023.

ETNEWS. (2023). *Renewable energy share exceeds 10%. On track to break record this year (신재생 에너지 비중, 10% 넘는다. 올해 사상 첫 돌파 유력)*. https://www.etnews.com/20231222000137. Accessed 18 March 2024.

Green Climate Fund. (2023). *Projects portfolio*. https://www.greenclimate.fund/projects. Accessed 16 May 2023.

Korea Indicator. (2023). *Greenhouse gas emission (온실가스배출량)*. https://www.index.go.kr/unify/idx-info.do?idxCd=4288. Accessed 10 May 2023.

Maennel, A., & Kim, H.-G. (2018). Comparison of greenhouse gas reduction potential through renewable energy transition in South Korea and Germany. *Energies, 11*(1), 206. https://doi.org/10.3390/en11010206

ODA Korea. (2023). *ODA news (소식)*. https://www.odakorea.go.kr/statistic/main#/tileLayout. Accessed 18 March 2023

United Nations. (2023). *The climate crisis—A race we can win*. https://www.un.org/en/un75/climate-crisis-race-we-can-win. Accessed 10 August 2023.

CHAPTER 10

The Evolution of Research and Partnership Activities in Support of Urban Transformation: The EU's Research and Innovation Framework Programme

Hanna Kang, Moon Jung Kang, and Jooyeon Moon

Abstract Rapid urbanization has been interlinked with sustainability challenges, underscoring the urgency of urban transformation. The EU has established financing initiatives to drive urban transformation actions, including through its research and innovation (R&I) funding programme. Employing a social network analysis approach, this study investigates shifts in partnerships within the programme. In particular, the study's relevance is noteworthy in light of the EU–Republic of Korea (hereafter referred to

H. Kang (✉) · M. J. Kang · J. Moon
National Institute of Green Technology KOREA, Seoul, Republic of Korea
e-mail: hkang@nigt.re.kr

M. J. Kang
e-mail: kangmj@nigt.re.kr

J. Moon
e-mail: jooyn.moon@nigt.re.kr

S. Klingebiel et al. (eds.), *Emerging Trends in International Development and Climate Policy*,
https://doi.org/10.1007/978-3-031-65671-2_10

as Korea) Green Partnership established in May 2023, and therefore have implications for the forging of impactful green collaborations between the EU and Korea.

Keywords Urban sustainability transformation · Research partnership · EU research and innovation framework programme · Social network analysis · EU-ROK Green Partnership

Introduction

Global population shifts towards urban areas have led to the issue of rapid urbanization becoming more prominent within discourse on sustainability. A sustained global trend of urbanization is anticipated, with the percentage or the population living in urban areas expected to increase from 56% in 2021 to 68% by 2050 (UN Habitat, 2023). Cities are the pivotal geographical units that concentrate economic activity, enable rapid technology deployment and enhance social diversity (SDSN, 2013). This transformative force of urbanization could be used to accelerate global sustainable development (UN Habitat, 2016). At the same time, the environmental impact of rapid urbanization, marked by increased pollution, resource depletion and habitat destruction, underscores the urgency of incorporating sustainable practices into urban development.

The influence of urbanization extends across diverse sociocultural, political, environmental and economic dimensions, fostering interactive processes that hold the potential for realigning urban systems towards sustainability. These dimensions encompass urban society, ecology, technology and infrastructure, urban culture and lifestyle, as well as governance and institutional frameworks (Frantzeskaki et al., 2017; Rotmans, 2006). Cities have evolved into spatial frameworks where these realignments actively unfold, constituting a process referred to as "transformation"—a fundamental shift towards sustainability (Frantzeskaki et al., 2017; Wolfram & Frantzeskaki, 2016).

In light of this understanding, the collaborative nature of contemporary research endeavours transcends traditional boundaries, engaging diverse stakeholders from research organizations, the private sector and civil society. Research partnerships emerge as catalysts for holistic and effective urban sustainability transformations, directly addressing the multifaceted challenges faced by cities worldwide and seeking innovative solutions through optimal synergies. The integration of innovative technologies and practices facilitated by these partnerships propels the adoption of smart infrastructure and green innovations in urban landscapes. Importantly, their influence extends to policy development, where research findings advocate for informed decision-making, influencing the prioritization of sustainability in urban planning. The global networking facilitated by these collaborations becomes a conduit for sharing experiences and best practices, contributing to a collective understanding of urban sustainability and fostering the adoption of successful models across diverse contexts.

The EU has instituted funding initiatives to propel actions for urban transformation, including through its research and innovation framework programme. This chosen focus stems from a recognition that collective efforts in science, technology and innovation are critical for the EU's progress and competitiveness. Contributing to the broader integration agenda of the EU, collaborative initiatives seek to break down barriers, promote knowledge exchange and foster a sense of shared purpose among member states. The programmes contribute to building a robust innovation ecosystem, supporting startups, fostering entrepreneurship and facilitating the transfer of research findings into practical applications (EC [European Commission], 2021).

Against this backdrop, the study aims to delve into the evolution of partnerships within research networks of the EU research and innovation framework programmes. Specifically, it scrutinizes the dynamic landscape of research collaborations in the thematic realm of urban transformation across the seventh Framework Programme for research funding (FP7) (2007–2013) and its successor Horizon 2020 (2014–2020), providing a temporal comparison to unveil partnership shifts. Through a critical examination of the EU's involvement in a total of 193 urban transformation projects, this study attempts to contribute to an understanding of successful strategies and collaborative cases, setting the stage for more informed and impactful initiatives in urban transformation and sustainable development, transcending geographical boundaries.

Analysis of the EU-Funded Research and Innovation Projects in Urban Transition

Methodology and Data

Social network analysis (SNA) was used to explore urban research projects in FP7 and Horizon 2020, revealing the complex connections in networks composed of nodes (individuals/entities) and ties (connections). SNA goes beyond descriptive statistics, offering insights into qualitative aspects of organizational collaboration, such as resource flows and relational dependencies. Various metrics were employed to characterize network connections, including network size, average degree and centrality. Centrality emerged as a crucial concept, influencing overall network structure and functionality. The degree of centrality, a well-established measure, quantifies the number of direct relationships a node maintains. This study also analysed "ego-centric networks" (Batallas & Yassine, 2006), providing insights into partnership behaviours at the level of the individual organization.

The ego-centric approach is applied in this study to evaluate the partnership behaviours of an individual organization's network: a research institution (the central node) and the neighbours directly connected to it (the alters) (Everett & Borgatti, 2006). It also clarifies the local circumstances and variations in the behaviour of individual research organisations.

The research focuses on analysing 193 R&I projects in the field of urban research that were funded by the EU between 2007 and 2020 (Table 10.1). The data used in this study were sourced from a publicly available official project database of the EU called CORDIS. To assess changes in project partnerships for different periods, we compared the networks formed by the relevant projects from two different phases: the FP7 spanning 2007 to 2013, and the Horizon 2020, covering 2014 to 2020. This study selected projects, the objectives of which include the keywords "urban", "city" or "cities", "regions", and "community". Consequently, 73 projects on the urban research were extracted from 501 projects under the "environment (including climate change)" section of the FP7, whereas 120 projects were extracted out of 762 projects under the "Climate action, environment, resource efficiency, and raw materials" section of the Horizon 2020.

Table 10.1 Description of EU-funded urban research project data used for the network analysis

Division	*FP7*	*Horizon2020*
Number of projects	73	120
Number of organizations	809	1,865
Number (proportion) of organizations	809 (100%)	1,865 (100%)
• EU countries	531 (65.6%)	1,572 (84.3%)
• Non-EU countries	278 (34.4%)	293 (15.7%)
Number (proportion) of organizations	809 (100%)	1,865 (100%)
• Research institutions	251 (31.0%)	320 (17.2%)
• Higher education institutions	217 (26.8%)	289 (15.5%)
• Private companies	216 (26.7%)	617 (33.1%)
• Public organizations	83 (10.3%)	371 (19.9%)
• Others	42 (5.2%)	268 (14.4%)

Source Authors' own creation

Statistical analyses were conducted to discern trends in the types of participating institutions. Overall, the number of projects focused on urban transformation increased by over 60% from 73 in FP7 to 120 in Horizon 2020, while the number of participating institutions surged from 809 to 1,865. The number of projects increased by 1.6 times, while the participation of institutions saw a 2.3-fold increase during the same period, implying that EU-supported urban research projects have evolved into more extensive endeavours, conducted through larger research networks.

The quantity of urban projects and organizations has expanded, and the type of collaborating entities has diversified, whereas the networks tend to be dominated by EU countries. Examining the proportion of project participation by organizational type, FP7 was predominantly led by research institutions or universities. In Horizon 2020, there was an upswing in business participation, accompanied by increased involvement from public and other institutions. This shift indicates a significant diversification in the network composition, which was previously dominated by research institutions. Conversely, as networks transitioned from FP7 to Horizon 2020, the participation of EU country-affiliated institutions notably increased, leading to a decrease in the involvement of organizations from non-EU countries.

Organizational data for each project consortium were collected and presented in a two-mode binary matrix that captures relationships between nodes and events. This matrix interprets projects as affiliated relationships, indicating the presence or absence of an organization's involvement in a project with 1 or 0, respectively. To facilitate analysis, a two-mode matrix was transformed into a one-mode-valued matrix based on the actors, illustrating the distribution and strength of partnerships between organizations through projects, enabling the utilization of various SNA techniques using UCINET.

Network Analysis

The examination of the overall network properties of EU-funded urban research projects (Table 10.2) unveiled a noteworthy shift: while the average degree of each organization increased from 25.11 to 34.85, the overall density of the network decreased. This transformation was accompanied by a rise in the number of components and a leaning towards fragmentation. This dynamic suggests an augmentation in the frequency of connections between research institutions, an expansion in the network size, and the emergence of diverse players. However, the substantial increase in the number of organizational islands, devoid of interconnections, implies that the exchange of information and expertise did not diffuse uniformly across the entire network but rather remained confined within specific clusters.

Moreover, the observed trend of increasing fragmentation, as indicated by the proportion of pairs of nodes unable to reach each other, serves as compelling evidence of a significant disconnection in mutual connectivity. This study provided a visual representation of the overall network structure, enabling the observation of patterns in urban research projects. In

Table 10.2 Overall network properties of the EU-funded urban research projects

Properties	*FP7*	*Horizon2020*
Number of projects	73	120
Number of organizations	809	1,865
Relations (Ties)	20,314	64,994
Average Degree	25.11	34.85
Density	0.0311	0.0187
Components	1	13
Fragmentation	0	0.0266

Source Authors' creation

Fig. 10.1, node colour denotes the type of entities, while node shapes convey additional information about the affiliation of institutions. The size of the circle (nodes), captions and thickness of the lines represent the absolute number of connections; larger circles and letters indicate nodes with more connections. The network connections were refined to highlight robust partnerships, focusing specifically on those with more than three connections.

Consequently, under FP7, EU universities played a prominent role, whereas the results for Horizon 2020 indicate increased participation from various types of institutions, including those classified as other entities. These other entities encompass initiatives, networks, NGOs, etc., capable of driving local implementation of urban research and engaging regional governments committed to sustainable urban development. Despite the emergence of numerous active and diverse organizations, it is notable that powerful core institutions with a high degree of centrality have emerged. Horizon 2020, in contrast to FP7, reveals centrally positioned institutions not only among universities and research centres but also among other entities and companies. For instance, within Horizon 2020, ICLEI is identified as the institution with an exceptionally large node size, signifying the highest degree of centrality. Additionally, circular nodes continued to dominate, underscoring the continued leadership of EU institutions. In summary, the significant aspects in Horizon 2020

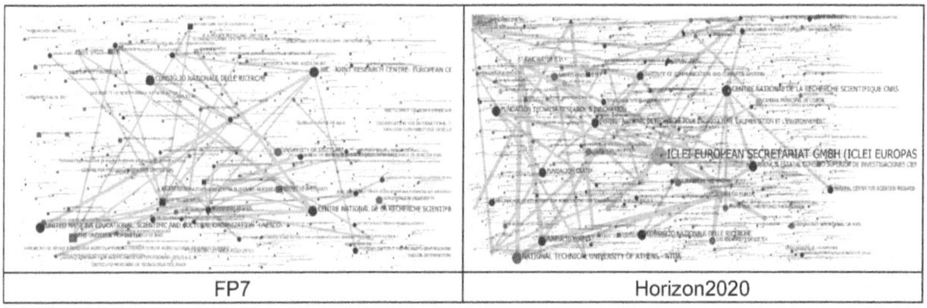

Fig. 10.1 Overall network structure (Cutoff of the relations > 2) (*Source* Authors' own creation. *Note* Colour legend: RED—Research sector, YELLOW—Private sector, ORANGE—Public sector, BLUE—Higher education sector, GREEN—Others/Shape legend: CIRCLE—EU countries, RECTANGLE—Non-EU developed countries TRIANGLE—Non-EU developing countries)

are the dominance of the EU institutions and the emergence of diverse organizations with a high degree of centrality.

This study investigated the top-10 degree-central organizations in urban research projects conducted under FP7 and Horizon 2020, analysing their characteristics (see Table 10.3). The results showed that in FP7 the most influential organizations were primarily universities or research institutes in both EU and non-EU developed countries in the EU region, such as the UK and Norway. In contrast, Horizon 2020 included a diverse mix of industry, academia and other NGOs in the EU region. Within FP7, numerous key central organizations occupied top-ranking positions, demonstrating consistently high centrality values. In contrast, the landscape shifted in Horizon 2020, where ICLEI's centrality value distinctly outshone that of other entities.

In summary, while FP7 urban research networks were characterized by active collaboration among multiple central organizations, Horizon 2020 presented a more unequal and hierarchical pattern, with one outstanding organization leading urban research. However, it is crucial not to oversimplify Horizon 2020 as centrally concentrated, as an examination of the overall network reveals a fragmented structure, with various isolated networks, contrasting with the more cohesive nature of FP7 networks.

In examining the ego networks of the most degree-central organizations in both FP7 and Horizon 2020 in Fig. 10.2, we observed noteworthy trends. The most influential organization in FP7, Joint Research Centre (JRC), predominantly engaged in collaborations with universities across both EU and non-EU developed countries. In Horizon 2020, ICLEI expanded its collaborative efforts to encompass a more diverse spectrum of EU organizations across different sectors. This observed shift in behaviour patterns among central organizations aligns with insights derived from the comprehensive analysis of the overall network structure.

Within the framework of the European Union's urban research network, we explore the dynamics of collaboration with non-EU entities. A scrutiny of the foundational statistics in Table 10.4 reveals that, among the 809 organizations participating in 73 FP7 urban research projects, 319 were non-EU entities, constituting 39.4% of the total. In contrast, under Horizon 2020, where 1,865 organizations engaged in 120 projects related to urban research, the number of non-EU entities notably decreased to 293, representing only 15.7% of the total. However, delving into the intricacies of EU–non-EU partnerships using descriptive analysis in Table 10.5 unveils a nuanced pattern.

Table 10.3 List of the most degree-central organizations

Rank	FP7				Horizon 2020			
	Organization name	*Type*	*Country*	*Value*	*Organization name*	*Type*	*Country*	*Value*
1	Joint Research Centre (JRC) (European Commission)	REC	BE	0.0579	ICLEI European Secretariat GmbH	OTH	DE	0.0503
2	Centre National de la Recherche Scientifique (CNRS)	REC	FR	0.0560	National Technical University of Athens (NTUA)	HES	EL	0.0320
3	United Nations Educational, Scientific and Cultural Organization (UNESCO)	REC	FR	0.0557	Centre National de la Recherche Scientifique (CNRS)	REC	FR	0.0307
4	Consiglio Nazionale delle Ricerche (CNR)	REC	IT	0.0554	Fundacion Tecnalia Research & Innovation	REC	ES	0.0279
5	The University of Exeter	HES	UK[a]	0.0473	Consiglio Nazionale delle Ricerche (CNR)	REC	IT	0.0274
6	University of Stuttgart	HES	DE	0.0439	Agencia Estatal Consejo Superior de Investigaciones Cientificas	REC	ES	0.0270
7	Wageningen University	HES	NL	0.0405	Fundacio Eurecat	REC	ES	0.0260
8	Stiftelsen SINTEF	REC	NO[a]	0.0381	Institut National de la Recherche pour l'Agriculture, l'Alimentation et l'Environnement	REC	FR	0.0251

(continued)

Table 10.3 (continued)

Rank	*FP7*				*Horizon 2020*			
	Organization name	*Type*	*Country*	*Value*	*Organization name*	*Type*	*Country*	*Value*
9	Potsdam Institut für Klimafolgen-forschung	REC	DE	0.0331	Fundacion CARTIF	REC	ES	0.0249
10	Bureau de Recherches Géologiques et Minières	REC	FR	0.0325	KWR Water B.V	PRC	NL	0.0242

Source Authors' own creation
[a]non-EU countries

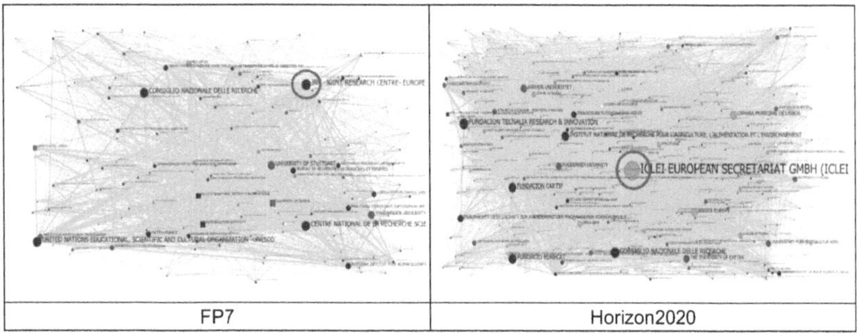

Fig. 10.2 Ego-network structure of the highest degree-central organizations (JRC and ICLEI) (*Source* Authors' own creation. *Note* Colour legend: RED—Research sector, YELLOW—Private sector, ORANGE—Public sector, BLUE—Higher education sector, GREEN—Others/Shape legend: CIRCLE—EU countries, RECTANGLE—Non-EU developed countries TRIANGLE—Non-EU developing countries)

Table 10.5 presents a compilation of the Top-5 highly engaged EU organizations in collaboration with non-EU partners. These EU entities, characterized by the highest number of collaborations with non-EU countries, serve as "gatekeepers", facilitating the entry of organizations from non-EU nations into the EU R&I network. A closer examination reveals that, in both FP7 and Horizon 2020, the most active organizations were predominantly research institutes or higher education institutions,

Table 10.4 Overview of the EU-funded urban research projects in collaboration with non-EU countries

Division	*FP7*	*Horizon2020*
Number of projects	73	120
Number of organizations	809 (100%)	1,865 (100%)
Number of non-EU organizations	319 (39.4%)	293 (15.7%)
Non-EU developed countries	137 (16.9%)	105 (5.6%)
Non-EU developing countries	182 (22.5%)	188 (10.1%)

Source Authors' own creation

with the exception of ICLEI, which, as a network, has the status of a non-governmental organization. Additionally, the degree-central EU institutions mentioned earlier exhibited strong collaboration performance in terms of the absolute number of collaborations with non-EU entities.

Conversely, organizations from non-EU countries with the highest number of collaborations with EU organizations can be interpreted as proactive "representatives" of non-EU countries seeking entry into the EU R&I network. In FP7, the list of highly engaged non-EU organizations collaborating with EU partners was largely dominated by institutions located in the EU region but not EU member states, such as Norway, and Switzerland, occupying the top five positions. In contrast, under Horizon 2020, institutions from Norway and Switzerland maintained positions in the top-5, and two Turkish universities emerged, highlighting a significant presence in the EU urban research network. These transformations are tied to the agreement on Turkey's joining Horizon 2020 in June 2014, granting association status to research entities from Turkey (EC, 2014). To summarize, within the EU urban research network, although the absolute number of participations by non-EU entities has decreased, the prominence of central collaborating institutions outside the EU region suggests a strengthening of substantive collaboration with the third countries.

This evolution in the behaviour of central organizations and the diversification of the EU's urban research network can be linked to emerging trends in response to diverse societal challenges within the field of urban research. The transformation reflects a need to understand and address the multi-dimensional societal issues inherent in urban research. Recognizing the complexity of these challenges, involving stakeholders from various sectors becomes pivotal. This shift in organizational collaborations may

Table 10.5 List of high-engagement organizations in EU–non-EU partnerships

	FP7				*Horizon2020*			
	The list of highly engaged EU organizations in collaboration with non-EU partners							
	Organization name	*Type*	*Country*	*Value*	*Organization name*	*Type*	*Country*	*Value*
1	United Nations Educational, Scientific and Cultural Organization (UNESCO)	REC	FR	84	ICLEI European Secretariat GmbH	OTH	DE	58
2	Joint Research Centre (JRC) (European Commission)	REC	BE	76	Centre National de la Recherche Scientifique (CNRS)	REC	FR	46
3	Centre National de la Recherche Scientifique (CNRS)	REC	FR	73	Universitaet fuer Bodenkultur Wien	HES	AT	45
4	Consiglio Nazionale delle Ricerche (CNR)	REC	IT	63	Wageningen University	HES	NL	39
5	University of Stuttgart	HES	DE	51	Aarhus Universitet	HES	DK	36
	The list of highly engaged non-EU organizations in collaboration with EU partners							
	Org Name	Type	Country	Value	Org Name	Type	Country	Value
1	The University of Exeter	HES	UK	94	SINTEF AS	REC	NO	96
2	Stiftelsen SINTEF	REC	NO	85	Norges Forskningsrad	PUB	NO	80
3	Meteorologisk Institutt Universite de Geneve	REC HES	NO CH	61	Union Internationale pour la Conservation de la Nature et de ses Ressources	REC	CH	75

(continued)

Table 10.5 (continued)

	FP7				*Horizon2020*			
	The list of highly engaged EU organizations in collaboration with non-EU partners							
	Organization name	*Type*	*Country*	*Value*	*Organization name*	*Type*	*Country*	*Value*
4	International Water Association LBG Oslo Kommune	REC PUB	UK NO	59	Izmir Institute of Technology	HES	TR	68
5	King's College London	HES	UK	58	Middle East Technical University	HES	TR	65

Source Authors' own creation

be attributed to the necessity of addressing the evolving and diverse societal challenges surrounding urban research, prompting EU institutions to diversify their partnerships over time.

This trend aligns with previous urban studies that emphasize the contributions of various stakeholders in urban areas. Stakeholders in urban environments possess diverse knowledge crucial for context-specific solutions that enhance sustainability (Reed, 2008; Soma et al., 2018). Additionally, the United Nations' New Urban Agenda (UN, 2017) underscores the need for broad cross-sectoral and cross-level integration as a fundamental requirement for policy and institutional change.

Case Study

This research examines the changes in network patterns through a case study analysis, focusing on two projects: the HEREPLUS project under FP7 and the ARCH project under Horizon 2020. These projects feature the participation of the most degree-central EU institutions, JRC and ICLEI, alongside non-EU institutions. Both endeavours are dedicated to exploring complex challenges within the urban context, with a specific emphasis on addressing issues such as air pollution and risks to cultural heritage.

Table 10.6 Partnerships and collaboration of HEREPLUS under FP7

Type	*Organization*
Research organizations	(Germany) Technische Universitaet Dresden (Belgium) JRC—Joint Research Centre—European Commission (Italy) Consiglio Nazionale Delle Ricerche (Spain) Instituto de Salud Carlos III
Higher Education	(Italy) Universita Degli Studi Di Roma la Sapienza (Greece) Academy of Athens (Serbia) Faculty of Medicine, University of Belgrade (UK) University of Keele Royal Charter

Source EC Cordis

FP7: Health Risk from Environmental Pollution Levels in Urban Systems (HEREPLUS)

The FP7-funded HEREPLUS project is dedicated to comprehending the crucial link between deteriorating urban air quality and cardio-respiratory diseases, focusing specifically on pollutants such as ozone and particulate matter. The research is centred in major European urban areas, utilizing GIS technology to develop comprehensive risk maps and models concerning human health, pollutants and ozone concentrations (Table 10.6). The consortium, notable for its diversity, forms a collaborative network involving research organizations and higher education institutions across various European countries. Importantly, the inclusion of the University of Belgrade from Serbia, a non-EU member state situated in the east-European region, underscores the project's commitment to international knowledge exchange in the field of urban research.

Horizon 2020: Advancing Resilience of Historic Areas Against Climate-Related and Other Hazards (ARCH)

The Horizon 2020-funded ARCH project is dedicated to enhancing the resilience of historic areas against climate-related and other hazards. ARCH focuses on chronic stresses and acute shocks, considering unique aspects of historic areas such as physical, environmental, economic, social, cultural and political factors. The project collaborates with pilot cities, including Bratislava, Camerino, Hamburg and Valencia, to design models, methods, tools and datasets for decision-making and resilience enhancement (Table 10.7). The consortium of ARCH under Horizon 2020 reflects a diverse collaboration pattern, bringing together research organizations, higher education institutions and other entities from multiple countries. Notably, the project includes the participation of Korea, a non-EU member state, represented by the Electronics and Telecommunications Research Institute. This international involvement highlights the project's commitment to a global perspective and the exchange of expertise beyond the EU borders.

These two projects were selected and analysed as examples of tasks in which projects with the most degree-central institutions participated during the FP7 and Horizon 2020 periods, and non-EU institutions were also part of the consortia. While serving as specific instances, they effectively showcase the evolution of the urban research collaboration network from FP7 to Horizon 2020. In the case of the FP7 project, HEREPLUS, the network predominantly centred on universities and research institutions within the EU region, with limited participation from non-EU institutions. However, the non-EU institution that was part of the project was in the broader European area. Conversely, the Horizon 2020 project, ARCH, demonstrated a more dynamic participation pattern, encompassing not only research institutions and universities

Table 10.7 Partnerships and collaboration of ARCH under Horizon 2020

Type	*Organization*
Research organizations	(Spain) Fundacion Tecnalia Research & Innovation (Italy) Agenzia Nazionale per le Nuove Tecnologie (Italy) Istituto Nazionale di Geofisica e Vulcanologia (Ireland) Research for Science, Art and Technology (RFSAT) Limited (Slovakia) Mestsky Ustav Ochrany Pamatok (Korea) Electronics and Telecommunications Research Institute
Higher education	(Italy) Universita degli Studi di Camerino (Slovakia) Univerzita Komenskeho v Bratislave
Other	(Germany) ICLEI European Secretariat GmbH (Germany) DIN Deutsches Institut fuer Normung EV (Spain) Fundacion de la Comunitat Valenciana para la Promocion Estrategica el Desarrollo y la Innovacion Urbana

Source EC Cordis

but also other organizational types such as non-governmental organizations and associations. Notably, a Korean research institution from a non-EU country actively engaged in the project. This implies that over time, the EU-funded urban research has transformed from collaborative research primarily for academic advancement to socially impactful research addressing societal issues, embracing a multifaceted approach through the involvement of various stakeholders.

Conclusion

The study explored the evolution of partnerships in the thematic domain of urban transformation across FP7 (2007–2013) and Horizon 2020 (2014–20). Utilizing social network analysis, the research scrutinized the network structure involving 7,955 organizations in 1,263 projects, offering a temporal comparison to reveal partnership shifts.

The findings revealed that urban research networks under FP7 thrived on active collaboration among several central organizations, fostering a more egalitarian structure. In contrast, Horizon 2020 displayed a more hierarchical pattern, with a singular organization taking the lead in urban research. It is essential, however, not to oversimplify Horizon 2020 as centrally concentrated. An analysis of the entire network exposes a fragmented structure with numerous isolated networks, a departure from the more cohesive nature observed in FP7 networks. In addition, EU-funded urban research has evolved from predominantly academic collaboration in FP7 to a socially impactful research model in Horizon 2020, emphasizing a broader engagement with various stakeholders to address societal issues.

The shift in the behaviour of central organizations and the broadening scope of the EU's urban research network are in line with emerging trends focused on tackling varied societal challenges within urban research. This shift emphasizes the importance of involving stakeholders from diverse sectors (public and private, research, civil society, etc.) to grasp and address the multifaceted societal issues inherent in urban research. The alteration in how organizations collaborate over time is a response to the urgent need to address evolving and diverse societal challenges, leading EU institutions to diversify their partnerships.

To further amplify this positive trajectory, the European Union (EU) and the Republic of Korea (ROK) jointly initiated a significant bilateral Green Partnership, a milestone achieved during the EU-ROK Summit on May 22, 2023 (EC, 2023). This landmark move not only marked the commencement of negotiations for Korea's association with Horizon Europe but also underscored a profound commitment to deepening collaboration in science and innovation. The comprehensive dedication extends to augmenting investments in research and development, fostering collaborative endeavours and facilitating the fluid mobility of researchers. As the study findings underscore the critical need for diversified partnerships across geographical boundaries and sectors involving diverse stakeholders, the Green Partnership emerges as a potent tool for fostering alliances between the EU and Korea. Urban innovations, in particular, become pivotal in this collective endeavour, reinforcing cooperation on various sustainability fronts, including climate policies, the just and clean energy transition and green technology. To ensure the successful implementation of the Green Partnership and promote effective green cooperation, it is essential to identify common and strategic research agendas between EU member states and Korea.

References

Batallas, D., & Yassine, A. (2006). Information leaders in product development organizational networks: Social network analysis of the design structure matrix. *IEEE Transactions on Engineering Management, 53*(4), 570–582.

Borgatti, S. P., & Everett, M. G. (2006). A graph-theoretic perspective on centrality. *Social Networks, 28*(4), 466–484.

EC (European Council). (2014). *Turkey joins Horizon 2020 research and innovation programme.* https://ec.europa.eu/commission/presscorner/detail/en/IP_14_631. Accessed 18 December 2023.

EC. (2023). *EU–Republic of Korea Summit (Seoul, 22 May 2023)—Joint Statement (9573/23).*

EC Cordis. *Health risk from environmental pollution levels in urban systems.* https://cordis.europa.eu/project/id/212854\

European Commission. (2021). *Horizon Europe: Investing to shape our future.* https://research-and-innovation.ec.europa.eu/system/files/2022-06/ec_rtd_he-investing-to-shape-our-future_0.pdf. Accessed 24 November 2023.

Frantzeskaki, N., Broto, V. C., Coenen, L., & Loorbach, D. (2017). Urban sustainability transitions: The dynamics and opportunities of sustainability transitions in cities. In *Urban sustainability transitions* (pp. 1–20). Routledge.

Reed, M. S. (2008). Stakeholder participation for environmental management: A literature review. *Biological Conservation, 141*(10), 2417–2431.

Rotmans, J. (2006). A complex systems approach for sustainable cities. In Ruth, M. (Ed.), *Smart growth and climate change: Regional development, infrastructure and adaptation.* Edward Elgar Publishing Limited.

SDSN, UN. (2013). *The urban opportunity: Enabling transformative and sustainable development*. United Nations Sustainable Development Solutions Network.

Soma, K., Dijkshoorn-Dekker, M. W. C., & Polman, N. B. P. (2018). Stakeholder contributions through transitions towards urban sustainability. *Sustainable Cities and Society, 37*, 438–450.

UN (United Nations). (2017). Document A/RES/71/256. Resolution adopted by the General Assembly on 23 December 2016. 71/256. New Urban Agenda. http://habitat3.org/wp-content/uploads/New-Urban-Agenda-GA-Adopted-68th-Plenary-N1646655-E.pdf

UN-Habitat. (2016). *World cities report 2016: Urbanization and development: Emerging futures*. UN Habitat.

UN Habitat. (2023). *World cities report 2022: Envisioning the future of cities*. UN HABITAT.

Wolfram, M., & Frantzeskaki, N. (2016). Cities and systemic change for sustainability: Prevailing epistemologies and an emerging research agenda. *Sustainability, 8*(2).

CHAPTER 11

Private Sector Engagement Policies in South Korea: Challenges and Policy Recommendations

Eunju Kim

Abstract The Korean government recently announced a strategy for engaging the private sector in international development. There are expectations that this will attract innovative solutions with more financial resources, but, on the other hand, there are concerns that private companies will only focus on pursuing commercial interests without paying attention to the normative legitimacy such as private sector development in partner countries. There are also concerns that fragmentation will further deepen as ODA funds are divided due to mutual non-interference among various actors. Finally, this study discusses policy implications for Korean private companies to be development agents which are derived from the case of German private sector engagement.

Keywords Private sector engagement · Development agent · Commercial motivation · Fragmentation

E. Kim (✉)
Hansung University, Seoul, South Korea
e-mail: eunjukim@hansung.ac.kr

S. Klingebiel et al. (eds.), *Emerging Trends in International Development and Climate Policy*,
https://doi.org/10.1007/978-3-031-65671-2_11

Introduction

Participation of private companies in South Korea's international development cooperation has increased. There are three main reasons behind this trend, from both a normative and realist perspective. From the normative perspective, as the total amount of official development assistance (ODA) has increased since joining OECD/DAC in 2010, there are growing concerns that efforts should be made to improve the quality of aid projects. To improve the quality of aid projects, an increasing number of people recognize that it is necessary to incorporate innovative problem-solving methods through the participation of private entrepreneurs. Second, during COVID-19, private companies began to take an interest in environmental, social and governance (ESG) management, which involves taking a sustainable approach in addition to making profits. This led to more attention on improving the environmental and social problems of developing countries responsible for raw material production and primary processing within the global supply chain. On the other hand, from a realistic perspective, government ministries have emphasized to Korean companies, the benefits they can gain in terms of share of the domestic market by engaging in development cooperation. As part of an export-oriented economy, Korean companies are also willing to become involved in development cooperation as an opportunity to expand their export markets.

It is important, however, for private actors to be a development "agent" rather than simply using development cooperation as a means to achieving their own business objectives. To be a development agent, private companies need to define the purpose, activities and operating principles of the company by aligning it with development goals in partner countries (Blowfield & Dolan, 2014). This will ensure that the expertise and innovative knowledge and skills of private companies contribute to the development of the private sector in developing countries.

Against this background, this study will examine Korea's private sector engagement policies and major programmes by analysing its problems, and will then suggest implications for further improvement. In particular, it will refer to the case of Germany, as an example of relatively strong private sector engagement (OECD, 2016).

Private Sector Engagement Policies and Programmes in Korea

The participation of private companies in Korea's international development cooperation began around 2010. Before that, private companies participated in ODA projects, but they remained in the role of the implementers of those projects. Most of Korean companies' participation came about through the ODA procurement market and a bidding process. However, recently, the role of private companies in Korean development cooperation has changed, with a new strategy and programmes.

First, the South Korean government announced the private sector engagement strategy in November 2022, which tries to facilitate private investment through ODA and to strengthen various support for private companies. The government announced that it will expand private investment and financial support, and to this end, it plans to introduce blended finance and impact investment. In order to facilitate the participation of private companies, the Korean government plans to expand the innovative programmes of KOICA (Korea International Cooperation Agency) and strengthen the link between companies' ESG activities and ODA. In addition, it decided to strengthen consultation channels between the government and businesses for networking and sharing information (Government of Korea, 2022).

Second, KOICA, as the leading development agency, has tried to expand its partnership with private sectors. In 2010, KOICA introduced the "Global CSR Program" as a public–private partnership programme. However, in the early stages, most of the projects were carried out as corporate social responsibility (CSR). There was a tendency for private companies to conduct development cooperation projects only to increase the company's brand value in society (Sohn et al., 2014, p. 133). Later, a new model emerged in the context of creating shared value by linking development cooperation projects with the company's core values and main business model. For example, Samsung Electronics conducted a vocational training project for women in the electronics field in Ghana together with GIZ, the German development agency. As a vocational training project to foster workers in electronics production factories in Ghana, it was recognized as a new way for companies to participate in international development cooperation (KOICA, 2015).

Around 2015, KOICA launched a new programme to expand participation of private companies by recognizing them as major actors in development. It launched the Creative Technology Solution (CTS) programme to support startup companies with innovative technologies to solve development problems in developing countries. Since 2015, 108 projects have been implemented in 22 countries by developing 68 innovative solutions (KOICA [Korea International Cooperation Agency], n.d. a). For example, Dot developed a Braille clock using appropriate technology and distributed it to developing countries at a reasonable price. Enuma has distributed programmes for learning English and basic mathematics using tablets in East Africa, South Asia and Southeast Asia (KOICA, n.d. a). It provided valuable opportunities to the students who are out of school due to COVID-19. The Inclusive Business Solution (IBS) is a programme that enables companies to carry out business activities targeting the "bottom of the pyramid" market by providing solutions in developing countries. During 2010 to 2021, 130 companies implemented a total of 165 projects in 30 countries. As of 2022, 47 projects were in progress (KOICA, n.d. b). For example, there was a project that contributed to the development of Vietnam's handicraft industry and an increase in workers' income by strengthening the design and quality of Vietnamese handicrafts and providing new distribution channels by establishing a global online commerce platform (KOICA, 2023).

Since 2022, not only small and medium-sized enterprises (SMEs) but also large companies have been able to participate in development cooperation. In Korea, there were legal restrictions on the participation of large corporations in government procurement as a protective measure for SMEs. Because of this, global companies and large corporations could not participate in KOICA projects. However, by introducing the KOICA ESG Initiative project, KOICA and the large corporations have jointly discovered a model that can contribute to achieving the SDGs while complying with the ESG goals of the large corporations. For example, in 2022–2023, Samsung Electronics newly launched a project in Uganda to prevent electronic waste through smartphone upcycling, and SK Forestry started a project to prevent forest devastation in northern Vietnam and contribute to reducing greenhouse gases (KOICA, n.d. c).

Third, the Export-Import Bank, responsible for managing the Economic Development Cooperation Fund (EDCF) which provides loans to developing countries, has implemented public-private partnership projects to promote private sector participation. For example, it has tried to apply the principle to large-scale infrastructure development in developing countries by utilizing the financial resources, technology and expertise of private companies. So far, EDCF has provided USD 310 million in support of a total of four projects (total project cost of USD 1.67 billion) (Government of Korea, 2022). There are also projects that use blended financing by linking ODA loans and other export finance. For example, the Karian Dam construction in Indonesia is a large-scale infrastructure project in which the dam was constructed through EDCF loans, a head race was constructed through another economic cooperation fund, and the construction of a water purification plant was supported through another export financing (Government of Korea, 2022).

Fourth, public institutions under the Ministry of Commerce, Industry and Energy also began to participate in ODA. Korea Trade-Investment Promotion Agency (KOTRA) also began encouraging private companies to become involved in ODA with a new programme to support Korean private companies' activities in overseas markets. They mainly operate CSR programmes that allow Korean companies to enter the global market by donating products and services. For example, during the COVID-19 pandemic, there were cases of COVID-19 analysis equipment and diagnostic kits being donated to Kenya and Bosnia with the help of KOTRA, which later led to the export of diagnostic kits to these markets (Government of Korea, 2022).

Challenges: Commercial Motivation, Fragmentation and Mutual Non-Interference

Although private sector engagement strategies and programmes are being introduced, there are challenges as might be expected with the emergence of new actors.

First, although, at the policy level, government claimed normative legitimacy such as partnership and financing for development in partner countries, private companies actually get involved in ODA for commercial reasons. In the past, private companies were viewed simply as implementing bodies carrying out ODA through the procurement market, but recently there has been a change in the perception of them as partners *promoting* development cooperation. However, Korean companies are actually participating in development cooperation to utilize the government's ODA budget resources as a means to enter overseas markets (Kalinowski & Park, 2016). According to a survey of private companies that had participated in ODA, half of the respondents (50%) said that the motivation is "to explore overseas business opportunities" followed by 23% "to receive financial/budgetary support from the government" (Yi et al., 2023, p. 29). While government emphasized that the participation of private companies for private sector development in developing countries, Korean companies have strong commercial motivations which need careful consideration about this gap. Government ministries are also promoting the idea that ODA will help Korean companies expand overseas to persuade the Korean people. In this line, private companies should make efforts to become development agents by aligning the purpose and activities with development goals in partner countries.

Second, as the participation of private companies increases, Korea's aid governance has tended to become more fragmented. As a result, problems of duplication and inefficiency among implementing agencies are occurring even in the participation of private companies. In the past, governance was divided between the Ministry of Foreign Affairs and KOICA in charge of grants, and the Ministry of Strategy and Finance and the Export–Import Bank in charge of loans. However, recently, new organizations such as the Ministry of Trade, Industry and Energy, the Korea Trade-Investment Promotion Agency (KOTRA), the Ministry of Land, Infrastructure and Transport, and the Korea Overseas Infrastructure & Urban Development Corporation (KIND) have become involved in the administration of ODA. These government ministries and public institutions have close relations with private companies, while promoting their main function regarding industrial policy and infrastructure policy in Korea. The participation of such institutions that encourage companies to advance overseas is welcome in the sense of expanding the actors in the field of ODA, but there are growing concerns that they only serve to pursue domestic economic benefits rather than the mission of Korea's ODA policy for partner countries.

There has also been no significant progress in discussions related to the establishment of development finance institutions. Because developing countries have the greatest interest in foreign direct investment, ODA funds serve as a catalyst for other financing resources, such as export finance, guarantees and bonds. However, there are still discussions on the development finance institutions that will take charge of blended finance. While other countries are integrating aid agencies and development finance institutions, Korea is lagging significantly in establishing responsible organizations, which require urgent action.

Third, there are concerns that coordination and coherence will decrease as mutual non-interference becomes more prominent among private companies. Unlike in Germany, aid policies do not receive much attention from the public in South Korea. There is a tendency in Korea for the public to support ODA without sufficient understanding; this can lead to a quick erosion of support in the face of negative news (Kim & Kalinowski, 2020). Many private companies are participating in Korea's ODA with the aim of receiving government financial support, as was found in a survey (Yi et al., 2023, p. 29). Once they secure their own financial resources, there is little interest in what projects other actors are doing and whether development goals have been achieved. In policy studies, this kind of political dynamics can be described as "mutual non-interference", as one of the main characteristics of distribution policy (Lowi, 1972). When various actors participate, it is necessary to lessen inefficiencies by adjusting overlaps among them and creating synergy through mutual collaboration. However, it becomes increasingly difficult to pursue coordination and coherence if private companies do not work based on the agreed policy direction of ODA. In addition, although it has been revealed that many private companies in Korea are participating, not enough information is shared about specific projects being carried out. Therefore, additional efforts should be considered to strengthen cooperation through networks and information sharing among private companies.

Lessons from Private Sector Engagement in Germany

According to the OECD/DAC evaluation, Germany's private sector engagement strategies and programmes are recognized as being relatively better compared to other European donors (OECD, 2016). Also, Korea's international development cooperation can learn valuable lessons from the case of Germany, which has a similar aid governance system, divided into grants and loans. Therefore, this study proposes further improvement of Korea's policies on private sector involvement, drawing on lessons from German private sector engagement programmes.

First, Korea needs to make efforts to harmonize commercial interests with the purpose of development cooperation. Germany itself tried to enlarge private markets in developing countries for a long time with a strategy on private sector development, which was seen as an essential precondition for economic development (BMZ, 2013). In addition, it emphasized the engagement of SMEs by providing technologies and products from German SMEs to developing countries. Germany, which has strength in the field of vocational training, has also tried to enhance the capacity of workers in developing countries with an apprenticeship model to provide necessary labour force (OECD, 2016). There are lessons for Korea from Germany's case that the balance between private sector development in developing countries and commercial interests of private companies from the donor countries.

Second, it is important to continuously coordinate between a variety of agencies and actors. Aid governance in Germany is also fragmented, with the Federal Ministry for Economic Cooperation and Development (BMZ) leading the policy direction, which involves different ministries, while GIZ and KfW are responsible for technical and financial cooperation. Private consulting agencies are also participating because it is necessary to elicit cooperation from private companies.

Various support programmes and financial resources are available from government ministries, but it is difficult for companies to know which programme is right for their company. To overcome this, the Agency for Business & Economic Development (AWE) was established, the aim of which is to identify and provide appropriate information to private companies (Kim & Lee, 2022, p. 14). This organization will operate programmes under a new brand of "Partners in Transformation" from 2024, which emphasizes partnership for achieving social and environmental transformation (AWE [Agency for Business & Economic Development], no date).

Korea needs to learn from the German example how to coordinate with private entities by establishing new organizations and relevant partnership initiatives. Fortunately, KOICA, which is dedicated to grant aid, established a department responsible for corporate cooperation in 2022. However, the Korean government needs to respond more actively by establishing development finance institutions and make efforts to encourage more companies to participate by launching a new initiative for business partnership.

Third, it is important to cooperate with business associations, by providing information about business opportunities to solve development problems in developing countries. Based on the tradition of corporatism and the guild of merchants, industrial and business associations play a central role in each sector in Germany. There are business associations that support German companies in many developing countries as well as regional chambers of commerce in Germany. BMZ has a programme called "Business Scouts for Development" that sends experts with knowledge and expertise on developing countries to provide information to chambers of commerce (BMZ website, no date). They have become a link between the business industry and the development cooperation field. In Korea, a similar policy could be adopted, with experts on development cooperation providing advice to chambers of commerce or business associations (Kim & Lee, 2022, p. 14).

It is also necessary for private companies to share information with each other to raise awareness of development cooperation. The website of the Agency for Business & Economic Development (AWE) describes the social problems facing developing countries in the hope that private companies will come up with innovative solutions (AWE, no date). This can be an opportunity for development cooperation and business to sharing examples of other companies addressing development issues and simultaneously creating business opportunities. In this way, information sharing between private companies can also be an initial step for cooperation among the private companies (Kim & Lee, 2022, p. 15).

Conclusion

In Korea, participation of private companies has recently been emphasized in development cooperation. Although new policies are being introduced, more efforts are still needed to enable private companies to become development agents that align their business purposes and activities with the developmental goals. Against this background, this study analyses Korea's approach to identify current challenges and suggest policy implications based on the German practice.

As the participation of private companies increases in Korea, there is a conflict between normative legitimacy and commercial interests. To solve this problem, we can learn from cases where German SMEs contributed to the growth of private markets and workforce improvement in developing countries, with the priority on the development of private markets in developing countries.

There is also a problem of fragmentation becoming more severe as multiple actors participate in Korea. This study proposes to establish a new financial development institution or business partnership by taking on board lessons from the case of Germany, which established a separate supporting organization and business partnership to engage private companies.

Lastly, private companies can become a "development agent" that contributes to development cooperation in the long-term when they conduct business with a sufficient understanding of development cooperation. Therefore, there is a need for additional efforts to link business associations and development in Korea so that private companies can become more aware of development issues and find innovative solutions. Drawing lessons from Germany, it is also necessary to raise awareness that business and development can be linked by sharing information on successful cases—those that pursue development goals and business opportunities together.

References

AWE (Agency for Business & Economic Development). (n.d.). *Advisory services*. https://wirtschaft-entwicklung.de/en/. Accessed 27 November 2023.

AWE. (n.d.) *Business opportunities in emerging markets*. https://www.leverist.de/de. Accessed 27 November 2023.

Blowfield, M., & Dolan, C. S. (2014). Business as a development agent: Evidence of possibility and improbability. *Third World Quarterly, 35*(1), 22–42.

BMZ (Bundesministerium für wirtschaftliche Zusammenarbeit und Entwicklung). (n.d.) *Business scouts for development*. https://www.bmz.de/de/themen/privatwirtschaft/kammern-und-verbaende/business-scouts-for-development-70214. Accessed 27 November 2023.

BMZ. (2013). *Sector strategy on private sector development* (BMZ Strategy Paper 9/2013e). Berlin: BMZ.

Government of Korea. (2022). *Private sector engagement strategy*. https://www.odakorea.go.kr/core/file/viewFileDown?fileId=1683161149834KRBYFJNPI0YWY5WZ3BW3Y20PR8

Kalinowski, T., & Park, M. J. (2016). South Korean development cooperation in Africa: The legacy of a developmental state. *Africa Spectrum, 51*(3), 61–75. https://doi.org/10.1177/000203971605100303

Kim, E., & Lee, D. (2022). Policy tools for private sector engagement in development cooperation. *Korean Policy Sciences Review, 26*(1), 1–22.

Kim, H. N., & Kalinowski, T. (2020). Only shallow? Public support for development cooperation in South Korea. *Asian International Studies Review, 21*(2), 29–53. https://doi.org/10.16934/isr.21.2.202012.29

KOICA (Korea International Cooperation Agency). (n.d. a). *Creative Technology Solution (CTS)*. KOICA. https://www.koica.go.kr/koica_kr/960/subview.do. Accessed 27 November 2023.

KOICA. (n.d. b). *Inclusive Business Solution (IBS)*. KOICA. https://www.koica.go.kr/koica_kr/961/subview.do. Accessed 27 November 2023.

KOICA. (n.d. c). *KOICA's ESG Initiative*. KOICA. https://www.koica.go.kr/koica_kr/961/subview.do

KOICA. (2015). *Plan to support private sector development in Africa*. Presentation at the KIEP expert seminar (unpublished)

Lowi, T. J. (1972). Four systems of policy, politics, and choice. *Public Administration Review, 32*(4), 298–310.

OECD (Organisation for Economic Co-operation and Development). (2016). *Private sector peer learning—Country report: Germany*. OECD. https://web-archive.oecd.org/2016-11-07/418061-Peer-Learning-Country-Report-Germany.pdf.

OECD. (2023). *Bottlenecks to access SDG finance for developing countries*. Paris, OECD. https://www.oecd.org/g20/oecd-g20-bottlenecks-sdg-finance-developing-countries.pdf

Sohn, H. S., Park, B. K., & Kim, N. K. (2014). A study on Korean Public-Private Partnership (PPP) for international development cooperation: Focusing on KOICA's global CSR Program. *Journal of International Area Studies, 23*(2), 121–155.

Yi, J., Woo, C., & Choi, C. (2023). International development cooperation and private sector engagement: South Korean firms' perceptions and challenges for PSE from the neo-institutionalist perspective. *International Development and Cooperation Review, 15*(2), 21–27.

Index

S. Klingebiel et al. (eds.), *Emerging Trends in International Development and Climate Policy*,
https://doi.org/10.1007/978-3-031-65671-2

SPRINGER NATURE

GPSR Compliance

The European Union's (EU) General Product Safety Regulation (GPSR) is a set of rules that requires consumer products to be safe and our obligations to ensure this.

If you have any concerns about our products, you can contact us on ProductSafety@springernature.com

In case Publisher is established outside the EU, the EU authorized representative is:

Springer Nature Customer Service Center GmbH
Europaplatz 3
69115 Heidelberg, Germany

The manufacturer's authorised representative in the EU is Springer Nature Customer Service Centre GmbH, Europaplatz 3, 69115 Heidelberg, Germany. If you have any concerns regarding our products, please contact ProductSafety@springernature.com

Printed and bound by CPI Group (UK) Ltd, Croydon, CR0 4YY
01/10/2026
02225978-0013